DEPARTMENT OF EMPLOYMENT

Manpower Paper No. 14

INDUSTRIAL RELATIONS PROCEDURES

By Norman Singleton

LONDON: HER MAJESTY'S STATIONERY OFFICE 1975

© Crown copyright 1975
First Published 1975

Other titles in the series:
1   Company Manpower Planning
2   Cost Benefit Aspects of Manpower Retraining
3   Skilled Engineering Shortages in a High Demand Area
4   Absenteeism
5   The Reform of Collective Bargaining at Plant and Company Level
6   In Working Order: a study of industrial discipline
7   On the Quality of Working Life
8   Employment Prospects for the Highly Qualified
9   Women & Work: a statistical survey
10 Women & Work: Sex differences and Society
11 Women & Work: a review
12 Women & Work: overseas practice
13 New Patterns of Working Hours

ISBN 0 11 360693 1

Contents

		Page
Introduction		1
1	Procedures	1
2	Negotiating Procedures	8
3	Grievances and disputes	16
4	Disciplinary procedures	30
5	Procedures on other matters	45
6	The role of third parties in procedures	54
7	Commitment to use procedure	64
8	The contribution of procedures	75

Introduction

The material on which this booklet is based was gathered following a reference made on November 15 1972 by the Secretary of State for Employment asking the Commission on Industrial Relations for a report on industrial relations procedures for dealing with (a) grievances and disputes and (b) disciplinary matters arising in the course of employment.

The inquiries carried out during 1973 and 1974 in pursuance of this reference covered 12 major industries in the private sector and 10 major industries and services in the public sector. Discussions based on structured questionnaires were held at industry, intermediate and domestic levels. In addition current industry-wide procedure agreements, believed to cover over 75 per cent of those applying to 300 or more employees, and a selection of domestic procedure agreements were studied. Valued cooperation was received from joint bodies, from employers, from trade union representatives and from the Department of Employment.

It was not possible to complete the inquiry before the CIR was disbanded. The present booklet makes use of some of the original inquiry material as the basis for a short general review of the role of procedures in industrial relations. I have been greatly assisted by the store of information gathered by the original team and by the ideas which they contributed to its interpretation.

I have also had the benefit of critical comment from a number of my old colleagues in the Department of Employment and the Commission on Industrial Relations and from other friends engaged in the practice or study of industrial relations. This has resulted in a number of improvements for which I am grateful. Differing views were expressed about where the emphasis should be placed in analysing the essential nature of procedures. Should more weight be given to the significance of procedures as an index of the power relationship between employers and employees? Or should the constitutional role of procedures be more firmly expressed and championed? These questions illustrate how opinion about procedures reflects opinion about the nature of industrial relations. My own view is that the power factor is of critical importance in the process by which jointly agreed procedures are achieved and modified. What is achieved however is not merely some transient truce terms but a *modus operandi* which embodies the ideas and the commitment of the signatories. Both process and outcome are important. Power should be directed not only to creating procedures but to sustaining them.

I hope that the booklet will be of practical value though it is not a working manual for the installation of a kit of suitable procedures. The aim has rather been to analyse the nature and purpose of procedures, to illustrate their working in practice and to indicate how they can contribute to better industrial relations.

NORMAN SINGLETON
11 August 1975

1 Procedures

1   A procedure is an established way of carrying out some piece of business, the course to follow to reach a particular goal. People involved in a common enterprise need to have a common understanding about the procedures they are to follow to co-ordinate their efforts and to regulate their mutual relationships. Procedures are an essential part of the fabric of social organisation.

2   Procedures are expressed in their most manifest form in explicit rules but their effect is far more widespread and pervasive than that deriving from such conscious formulation. People progress along well-trodden procedural pathways with as little consciousness of following a procedure as Monsieur Jourdain had that he had been talking prose all his life. Awareness of the proper course to follow rests largely on habit, precedent and a common understanding of accepted custom and practice. Even written procedural rules may represent only a convenient formulation for reference and guidance rather than a type of regulation with attendant enforcement problems. The range of procedural arrangements from the explicit formal rules of august institutions to the accepted informal customs of day-to-day behaviour matches the variety and complexity of forms of social organisation.

3   Procedures may be laid down by authority or agreed between those who are going to abide by them. Their effectiveness does not necessarily correspond to their formal force but depends more on use and acceptability. Even provisions backed by legal authority are ineffective if they are either not invoked or are flouted with impunity. Procedures must be in reasonable conformity with the views of the generality of those who are to observe them if they are to condition the general pattern of behaviour.

4   Although procedures are concerned with method rather than substance the procedures adopted to deal with a new situation, or the interpretation applied to established procedures, can have a powerful influence on substantive issues. The first encounters in negotiations about substantive issues often take the form of arguments over procedural matters as can be seen in many international negotiations where agreement on procedure is the first item for discussion. Where procedural rules are well established and enjoy great authority they can often be turned to good account to serve purposes not in mind when they were originally devised. Reports of Parliamentary proceedings often give instances of notable ingenuity in

using established procedures to further particular policy aims. A good understanding of procedural possibilities is an essential part of the qualifications of practised advocates and negotiators.

5   A new procedure is shaped by the needs it is designed to meet and by the examples of how similar needs have been met elsewhere. Its effectiveness will depend in the first instance on the suitability of the original arrangements and subsequently on keeping a proper balance between adaptability to new needs and the maintenance of consistency and order in the handling of business. Established procedures can be adapted to meet new needs without formal amendment if the old provisions lend themselves to interpretations and applications which keep in step with changing actualities but this needs a high degree of mutual understanding on common objectives among those who operate the procedures. It is not only in their formal provisions but through their manner of operation that procedures have to be assessed.

6   The concept of a procedure is so integral to human actions in general that more specific meaning has to be sought either from the purpose to be served, e g a procedure for dealing with grievances — or from the areas where procedures have acquired a special significance. The dictionary definition of procedure makes particular mention of parliamentary and legal business and it is noteworthy that Parliament and the courts are institutions concerned with dealing with differences of opinion and interest. It is in the context of the resolution of differences that procedures have a role of particular importance by providing an accepted method of dealing with such business.

7   It is because of the need in a working community to provide orderly, consistent, known methods for dealing with working relationships, considering problems arising from them and resolving differences that procedures are of such central importance in industrial relations. In this context procedures are commonly thought of as those procedures which have been jointly agreed between managements and the representatives of their employees and it is on such procedures that this study will concentrate. But the basic needs for order, consistency and a general understanding of accepted ways of proceeding existed before the evolution of jointly agreed procedures and indeed exist today in establishments where trade unions are not recognised and procedures are determined solely by the management.

8   Jointly agreed procedures have evolved as a method of exercising what was originally regarded as solely a responsibility of the employer who prescribed the objectives of the organisation and the procedures for

attaining them. But of course even in an establishment where there is no recognition of trade unions and all procedures are laid down by the management the employer has to pay attention to the views of his employees if the procedural arrangements over which he may claim sole authority are to have the acceptability needed to ensure that the work is carried on. Acceptance of methods and procedures is needed to secure the co-operation required for the proper functioning of a working community. Jointly agreed procedures are a development which makes explicit provision to meet that need in the handling of those matters which affect the interests of employees.

9   Such procedures are not however merely a more efficiently organised way of ascertaining employee opinion in order to take it into account in the interests of the more successful operation of the enterprise. That is a management aim which is often pursued by *ad hoc* inquiry methods and various forms of staff committee systems and consultative arrangements. Under jointly agreed procedures there is a crucial change in the authority for deciding on procedural arrangements and for backing their operation. It ceases to be solely a management responsibility and becomes shared with representatives of the employees.

10   The recognition of a trade union is therefore a highly significant step. It is in form a renunciation of sole management authority in respect of the matters covered in the recognition agreement. Most commonly these relate to pay and conditions of employment but a recognition agreement is not an instrument for determining substantive pay and conditions. It normally lays down an agreed procedure by which they shall be determined. It is the first significant procedure agreement. It is however only the first step in the establishment of a negotiating relationship from which there can and commonly does develop a whole structure of jointly determined procedural arrangements. Once a trade union's claim to represent employee interests has been recognised the definition of the scope of those interests and of acceptable arrangements for handling them becomes the subject of continuing discussion between the parties. In any establishment where trade unions are recognised there are two authority systems consisting of all those aspects of running the business which are the normal and sole responsibility of the management and those aspects which have been made by agreement the subject of joint determination.

11   Such a twofold system is not the product of organisational theory but a response to pressures arising from the organisation of the workforce. Joint regulation seeks to reconcile the interests and viewpoints of management and employees by a process of negotiation but it begins with the recognition that there are such differences of interest and viewpoint and

that there is sufficient strength behind them to make the quest for agreement necessary and desirable. Agreed procedures establish a *modus vivendi* reflecting the interests and strength of the parties.

12 Joint regulation is not a static system. There is a tendency where negotiating relationships are successfully established for the area brought within the scope of joint determination to be constantly enlarged. Interpretations of what is comprised by pay and conditions broaden beyond what may have originally been conceived in narrow terms of basic rates and hours of work to include questions of manning and the pay system itself; productivity bargaining brings working methods and operational systems within the scope of negotiation; new subjects such as pensions may, through evolving changes of attitude and example, become accepted as proper for transfer from sole management determination to the area of joint determination. A good mutual understanding about currently accepted areas of joint responsibility and congruent views about evolution and change are both the signs and the products of good industrial relations.

13 The procedures which are established within such a relationship are far more than an arid formalism, a codification of agreed rules. They embody a common understanding about the appropriate way of dealing with matters in which both parties have an acknowledged interest. Much of that understanding may not be explicitly expressed in formal terms but be understood and accepted as custom and practice. For both parties a breach of procedure can be far more serious than an important difference over a particular substantive issue if it is seen as a breakdown of the arrangements embodying their mutually-agreed relationship. So for both parties maintenance of procedure becomes a policy aim in its own right.

14 A further limitation of sole management authority to determine procedures is accepted by those firms in membership of employers' associations which have entered into national procedural agreements with trade unions. Such agreements may provide principles and guidelines affecting domestic procedures within the firm and may in addition provide further procedural means outside the firm for dealing with issues which have not been resolved domestically. In some cases membership of an employers' association means that decisions on trade union recognition are not taken by the firm on the basis of representative capacity within the firm but are taken at national level and then become applicable within member firms. Nationally-negotiated procedure agreements have broader provisions and often a more restricted scope than can be found in a domestic procedure applying to a particular firm. They need to be supplemented by domestic procedures even if the sole purpose is to give a meaningful local interpretation to broad national provisions rather than to extend their scope.

15 Joint determination is one major distinguishing feature in analysing industrial relations procedures which may be further classified according to their scope and purpose. There are jointly-agreed procedures for the negotiation of wage settlements, for the resolution of disputes, for settling individual pay and grading issues, for dealing with individual grievances, for handling disciplinary cases, for reaching decisions on dismissals, for recruitment, for training, for redundancy and indeed for any class of business which is brought within the area subject to negotiation.

16 Such classifications help to bring a diffuse subject into closer focus but within each category there is great diversity. A detailed examination of particular local situations shows a variety of interpretation and practice between firms operating within the same nationally-agreed procedure. There are differences in the subjects accepted as being within the scope of domestic procedures and in the arrangements for dealing with the various items and differences in the degree to which the formally agreed arrangements correspond to actual accepted practice. There is constant movement to meet new situations and adapt to new ideas. Such diversity is only to be expected. The procedures governing behaviour at work are influenced by many factors. These include the size of the establishment, the nature of the work, the technology, the quality and style of the management, the extent of trade union organisation and all the personal, local and historical considerations which have helped to shape the accepted pattern and which condition the dynamics of change.

17 The following chapters report on some of the matters of importance to industrial relations which have been made the subject of jointly agreed procedures, give examples of how this has been done and comment on some of the implications of operating jointly agreed procedures.

2 Negotiating Procedures

18 The inquiries on which this study is based related primarily to grievance, disputes and disciplinary procedures. No systematic analysis was made of negotiating procedures and any attempt to give a comprehensive account of the forms and practices by which terms and conditions of employment are determined would be a major undertaking. A brief general reference is, however, essential. The determination of pay and conditions is so central to the relationship of employers and employees that it affects their mutual relations in many other respects. It is the practice of settling pay and conditions by negotiation which often leads to jointly agreed procedures covering other aspects of employment. Although no attempt is made in this chapter to examine negotiating procedures in detail some features are noted which are relevant to the general subject of jointly agreed procedures.

19 A procedural relationship between an employer and a trade union is established as soon as the union's right to represent the interests of its members is recognised. When that right includes the settlement of terms and conditions of employment by negotiation the active continuity of the relationship is maintained as adjustments are made to meet constantly changing circumstances. The procedural aspects of an act of recognition establishing negotiating rights are usually concerned with defining the area in respect of which the union's representative capacity is acknowledged, indicating the subjects which are brought within the scope of negotiation, the steps by which agreement is to be sought and the procedure to be followed if there is failure to agree. The basic procedures established at the outset are often elaborated in the subsequent stages of the practice of negotiation to fill in details, to make special provision for particular problems and to cover new subjects. This led the representative of one large firm, when invited by the Department of Employment to send in copies of current procedural agreements, to comment that he would have to supply a barrow-load of minutes of joint meetings extending over the past fifty years.

20 Procedures for settling pay and conditions by negotiation take many forms. Sometimes they are expressed in the formal provisions of the constitution of a joint council; often negotiations are carried out by means of *ad hoc* meetings hardly recognised as a procedure at all. Some procedure must, nevertheless, always follow a decision to negotiate. There has to be a way in which the negotiations are carried out which constitutes the negotiating procedure, however simple, however lacking in explicit formulation. In time, however, with the repetition of previous practice, with the adoption of methods for handling new problems as they are encountered, even the least sophisticated negotiating arrangements take on the character of an established procedure, the accepted method of conducting negotiations.

21   Advice of a general character on the form which negotiating procedures might take was contained in one of the reports of the Whitley Committee appointed in 1916 which recommended the establishment of Joint Industrial Councils. The report was followed up by the Ministry of Labour which drew up a Model Constitution and Functions of a Joint Industrial Council. Such councils were established in a number of industries but the Whitley recommendations were not adopted in many important industries which preferred to stick to the arrangements already established. In engineering for example there is no standing joint negotiating machinery though the establishment of such machinery has often been advocated by outside observers. There are well-established procedures for national discussion of pay and other matters between the Engineering Employers' Federation and the Confederation of Shipbuilding and Engineering Unions but they operate on an *ad hoc* basis and not through formal joint machinery. Joint Councils on the Whitley model were adopted and successfully developed in the Civil Service and local government and the extension of the public sector through the National Health Service and the nationalised industries has seen a big development of formally constituted joint negotiating machinery. Joint Industrial Councils have proved to be useful successor bodies to Wages Councils which have been abolished following the development of a sufficient degree of organisation to sustain collective bargaining.

22   The recommendations of the Whitley Committee were based on the concept of industry-wide negotiation of pay and conditions which came under criticism from the Donovan Commission on the grounds that over large areas pay and conditions were in reality determined at company or factory level. The Commission did acknowledge that in some areas, notably in the public sector, pay and conditions were effectively determined by national agreements and it is in these areas that the Whitley system is mainly found. Many of the Whitley ideas can however be adapted and applied to the creation of institutions at company or factory level for the negotiation of those comprehensive agreements on pay and conditions and on procedures for which the Donovan Commission called. Many companies have successfully developed such institutions.

23   In emphasising the need for negotiating arrangements at company and factory level the Donovan Commission based their recommendations on an

analysis of where and how pay is effectively determined. Negotiating procedures are intimately bound up with the pay system. In some large areas of employment, notably in the public services, all pay questions are dealt with centrally and the results applied uniformly through grading systems operating on a national basis; in other areas in both the public and private sectors pay is determined through a combination of national and local negotiations taking a wide variety of forms. Firms in membership of an employers' association have to take account of any nationally agreed provisions in their domestic arrangements for dealing with pay and conditions; within single companies which are not so affiliated and even within single establishments the contents of the pay packet may be the product of negotiations at different levels. The negotiating procedure may thus comprise a number of sets of negotiations, sometimes with a planned relationship but often quite unco-ordinated.

24 The pay system affects not only the form of negotiating procedures but has wider consequences for industrial relations. Where power to reach agreements is widely dispersed, as under some forms of piecework, the opportunities for inconsistency are multiplied. This in turn can affect the numbers, type and scale of disputes. The procedure for the resolution of disputes has to take account of their causes and special provision may need to be made for dealing with disputes about piecework prices. Where the pay system is so fragmented as to be out of control the burden of disputes may overwhelm an otherwise adequate disputes procedure.

25 The Donovan Commission saw the establishment of comprehensive bargaining machinery at company and/or factory level as the answer to the problems arising from the dispersal of bargaining authority between national and domestic levels and from its unco-ordinated dispersal within a company. The settlement of terms and conditions of employment was to be a first objective and the Commission expressed their belief that the establishment of such machinery would assist in the negotiation of pay structures which would be 'comprehensive, fair and conducive to efficiency.'

26 Alongside their recommendation on collective bargaining machinery to deal with terms and conditions of employment the Donovan Commission recommended as other objectives of company policy the establishment of agreed procedures covering grievances, discipline, redundancy and facilities for shop stewards and the promotion of joint discussion of safety measures. They did not recommend that the handling of all these subjects should be brought within the ambit of the comprehensive collective bargaining machinery which they advocated, although in discussing the merits of factory agreements they noted that a factory agreement could cover the constitution of the negotiating committee, pay methods and systems, and a whole range of procedures.

27 The inquiries showed a great variety of practice and opinion on two of the questions on which the Donovan Commission made no specific recommendation. First, should negotiating machinery be kept separate from consultative machinery? Secondly should the central negotiating machinery exercise a general jurisdiction over all matters which are subject to negotiation and joint agreement?

28 Those who advocate separate joint machinery for the purpose of consultation claim that there can be a fuller interchange of views over a wider range of subjects if it is clear at the outset that the discussion is free from any element of bargaining. Separate machinery for negotiation and consultation clearly establishes which matters are subject to joint regulation and encourages uninhibited discussion of other matters of common interest.

29 Those who advocate using the same joint machinery for negotiation and consultation do not deny that there are indeed some matters which are clearly subject to negotiation and others on which any interchange of views is purely consultative. They see the difficulty not in recognising that there are two processes but in trying to draw a sharp line between them emphasised through different institutional arrangements. Discussion of some subjects which starts as a consultative matter may raise issues which are accepted as negotiable. Other negotiable matters may sometimes be conveniently treated as consultative and merely noted. If negotiation and consultation take place with the same representatives of employees, the discretionary handling of such issues is most conveniently carried out in the same forum. If in addition to separate institutions for consultation and negotiation there are different systems of employee representation, the possibility of friction arising from the separation of the two processes is greatly increased.

30 A formal distinction between consultation and negotiation with separate machinery for the two purposes is found in a number of nationalised industries including railways, coal-mining and electricity supply. The institutions are well established and work well in practice largely because of the good understanding which the parties have developed in making the arrangements work. In the railways for example the written provisions do not permit reference to higher levels of issues arising at local level in the consultative machinery but as one union representative indicated, if a 'consultative issue' was particularly difficult to solve at local level and was likely to give rise to trouble then the means to discuss it at higher levels would be found. Management in two areas emphasised the importance of establishing good informal arrangements with local departmental committee representatives and exchanging information and views outside formal procedural channels. A clear distinction between negotiable and consultative issues was deemed to be difficult to maintain as illustrated by the closely connected subjects of staff complementing and rostering of which only the second was in theory negotiable.

31 The difference between consultation and negotiation may be clearly distinguished at the extremes but in the centre there is a good deal of shading and shifting. Where unions are strong and have established a powerful negotiating position consultations are often coloured by a strong negotiating element which may be implicit rather than overtly claimed or acknowledged. Formal distinctions which are found on occasion to constitute a barrier to reaching an understanding are often circumvented by informal methods. These reflections of the power situation were noted both in cases where the institutions for consultation and negotiation were separated and also in cases where they were combined. Examples of the successful operation of both systems were observed but with separate institutions the need to adapt theory to practice was more clearly apparent.

32 Practice and opinion varied not only about the use of negotiating machinery established at company or establishment level for consultation but also about its use as a central agency for the oversight and control of all matters which were the subject of jointly agreed arrangements. The answer was often dictated by practical considerations such as the size of the company and its operational structure, the number of unions involved and whether they were prepared to work together. Where however it is a practical possibility there are advantages in making the central negotiating machinery the focal point for the creation and oversight of agreed procedures. This makes for a fuller understanding of negotiating rights and responsibilities. It need not imply over-centralisation in the operation of procedures but can provide a means for achieving uniformity of general policy and for dealing with particular problems consistently.

33 The form of a negotiating procedure is expressed not only in the institutional arrangements but also in the practices developed for the processing of business. Like other procedures pay negotiations have strong ritualistic aspects. It is normal for an initial meeting to be devoted to the presentation of a claim and for the response to be deferred to a subsequent meeting. Often discussions extend over a series of meetings. Unduly protracted negotiations have often been criticised by inquiry bodies appointed to consider the causes and circumstances of disputes. Time is however an important element in the negotiating process and parties usually have a good mutual understanding as to how they use it. It can be used quite neutrally to make reasonable provision for examination of data and necessary consultation but it can also be used as a bargaining weapon either through delay or through forcing the pace. In the later stages of negotiation the pressure of time becomes a clearly recognised power factor. Procedures vary widely in the degree to which they attempt to programme negotiation but the management of time is always an important part of negotiating tactics. Complete discretion may be reserved by refusing a commitment to any programme at all. Where, as in the railways, the negotiating procedure provides for discussion through a succession of stages the parties accommodate their tactics and timing to the known procedural requirements.

34 Another important element in the negotiating process is the need for information. Discussion about maintaining or improving living standards creates a need for information on wage rates, earnings and price levels and more generally on economic trends and prospects; staffing structural requirements and a sense of equity direct attention to relativities both internal and external; the relationship of pay to economic performance raises issues of improving productivity.

35 Just as the time factor can be used neutrally or as a bargaining pressure in negotiations so information can play a neutral role of commonly accepted background fact or can be used as part of the process of advocacy through selection and interpretation. Both processes are normally present in negotiations but it makes for more useful discussion if fact can be distinguished from argument. Much relevant information on economic trends is available from neutral official sources but the parties can, by agreement, extend the area of uncontested fact. Some negotiating procedures, particularly in the public sector, make provision for the supply of such information. A notable example is found in the non-industrial Civil Service where a pay research unit under the joint control of both parties supplies them with a common fund of information about organisation, duties, pay and other emoluments in comparable employments.

36 The supply of information by employers to trade unions is a policy commended by government which in recent years has found expression in government measures. As a normal feature of the negotiating procedure it is in general much more commonly found in the public sector. Arguments advanced during the inquiries by employers who were reluctant to extend the provision of information included difficulties about confidentiality, the view that the negotiating process did not require one of the parties to help to advance the case of the other and the view that negotiations were essentially a matter of power bargaining to which information was of little relevance. Some trade union representatives also expressed sceptical views about the role which information plays in bargaining but in general trade unions felt that they were at a disadvantage in access to information and strongly favoured greater disclosure. Many employers thought that a ready supply of information could do much to improve understanding and lessen the area of contention though occasionally it was apparent that these views were based on a belief that full knowledge of all the facts could only result in acceptance of the management's interpretation of them.

37 The supply of information to improve the negotiating procedure is itself a suitable topic for negotiation and agreement. Information requirements vary between different industries and firms according to the matter which is under negotiation. When management and unions discuss what their information requirements are, how they might be met, how difficulties might be acknowledged or circumvented experience shows that acceptable procedures for the disclosure of information ancillary to the negotiating procedure can be made the subject of joint agreement.

38 Negotiating procedures are the creation of the parties who alone are competent to decide how they will conduct their negotiations but in the process they may seek the assistance, or have to accommodate themselves to the intrusion of a third party. In some cases, for example in national negotiations in the hosiery industry, a third party in the form of an independent chairman is present though this is not common. Third party intervention going beyond the parties immediately involved is provided by the external stages of nationally agreed procedures. In some cases provision is made to invoke third party assistance in the form of a conciliator in the event of failure to agree. Some procedures provide for the resolution of differences by recourse to arbitration but such arrangements normally depend on the agreement of the parties either *ad hoc* or in the form of a standing arrangement as in the Civil Service arbitration agreement.

39 Third party intervention is not however experienced solely as a result of agreed arrangements. For the three and a half million workers within the scope of Wages Councils the procedures for determining minimum terms and conditions of employment are laid down by Act of Parliament and provide for third party presence during discussions and third party enforcement of the outcome. Pay of workers within the scope of Wages Councils often depends also on local negotiations and the procedure for determining their pay includes both the work of the Council and the local settlements. In some cases national settlements reached by collective bargaining are brought to the Wages Council for formal endorsement. In such cases, the independent members of the Council have no effective part to play, the third party role consisting of the promulgation of the terms of the agreed settlement in a Statutory Order made by the Secretary of State for Employment and its enforcement by the Wages Council Inspectorate.

40 In recent years the long-established interest of the State in the wider results of disputes through the setting-up of independent inquiries has increasingly been extended to an interest in the wider results of agreements. Incomes policies are concerned with the results of negotiations rather than with the procedures by which the results are arrived at but incomes policies which provide for the notification and scrutiny of claims and settlements clearly have a direct impact on negotiating procedures. Guidance to negotiators on such matters as intervals between settlements, increments, merit awards, regradings and promotions may impinge on established procedures for dealing with these matters and may be met by procedural adjustments to take account of the new situation.

41 Third party intervention in negotiating procedures mostly arises when a dispute occurs or is threatened. Disputes procedures are examined in the next chapter and some aspects of third party intervention are considered in Chapter 6.

42 Negotiating procedures do not conform to standard patterns and cannot readily be stereotyped. Model procedures for the handling of disputes and grievances are more easily come by than model procedures for the conduct of negotiations. Advice on negotiating procedures is however available from employers' organisations, from trade unions and from the Advisory, Conciliation and Arbitration Service and negotiating procedure is an important item in industrial relations training courses.

43 All jointly-agreed procedures are the product of negotiation. For this reason the negotiating procedure can play a key role in the implementation of industrial relations policy if it is given a broad scope and made the effective co-ordinating centre for the creation and oversight of other jointly agreed procedures.

3 Grievances and disputes

44 Grievances and disputes procedures are grouped together to form one of the two kinds of procedures to be examined under the terms of reference for the inquiry which provided the basis for this report. A grievance procedure is commonly thought of as the method by which an individual raises some query or complaint about his or her pay or working conditions and the steps which are laid down for dealing with the matter. But a grievance can affect a group of individuals either in relation to working conditions e g the temperature in the workroom or in relation to matters affecting pay, such as the allocation of overtime or the grading of a group of employees.

45 A procedure for dealing with grievances is found both in companies and organisations which recognise trade unions and in many which do not. In the latter case the procedure has the characteristics of informing the individual of the action to be taken to raise a grievance and of the steps which the management will take to give it consideration. Where there is established negotiating machinery the arrangements for handling grievances are normally set up by joint agreement and the joint negotiating machinery may be involved as a part of the procedure if the grievance is not disposed of in the earlier stages of the prescribed arrangements.

46 An unsettled grievance can clearly give rise to a dispute and it was no doubt with this evolution in mind that grievances and disputes procedures were grouped together in the terms of reference. Disputes also occur however through failure to agree on matters which originate in the negotiating procedure. Negotiating procedures, as was noted in the last chapter, commonly provide for the steps to be taken in the event of failure to agree in negotiation, i e they may include a disputes procedure. A disputes procedure can therefore be a feature or element of both a grievance and a negotiating procedure though some joint factory committees with negotiating functions do not make specific provision for the resolution of disputes. In some cases negotiating and grievance procedures with their associated disputes provisions are kept separate; in others the disputes procedure is used to process issues arising either from general negotiations or from the operations of the grievance procedure. Sometimes no distinction is made between a negotiating procedure and a grievance procedure where all dealings with union representatives are regarded as a form of negotiation or alternatively where all such business, including the response to wage claims, is regarded as dealing with

grievances. Where there is a recognised distinction between negotiating and grievance procedures it may not be clear-cut in cases where the negotiating machinery is embodied as a stage in the grievance procedure or where an issue arising as a sectional grievance is adopted as the subject of a formal claim.

47 The variety of forms and practice in grievance and disputes procedures is matched by a rich variety in terminology. In some organisations the term 'grievance' is avoided altogether and instead 'complaint', 'issue', 'question', 'matter' or some other term is used. In some organisations grievances are associated only with individual employees, disputes only with groups of employees. In some organisations a grievance, whether individual or collective, is regarded as a dispute as soon as a shop steward is involved, in some cases when a full-time official of the union is called in. In some organisations a grievance only becomes a dispute if it is not solved at domestic level and is referred to an external procedure, whether company-wide or industry-wide. In some industries the term dispute is associated only with failure to agree or a breakdown in procedure. In the engineering industry, for example, the recently terminated procedure for manual workers was known as 'the procedure for avoiding disputes'.

48 It is a common feature of a grievance procedure that an aggrieved employee should have recourse to one or more levels of management. In the first instance he raises his grievance with his immediate superior. If it is not settled at that level he may take it to the next level of management and so on until it is resolved. It is essential to settle a grievance as near the point of origin as possible if the preventive character of the procedure is to be fully realised and the significance of the different procedural stages established and maintained.

49 In some of the cases studied the employee was expected in the first instance to go alone to his supervisor. If satisfaction was not obtained his shop steward could take the matter up with the supervisor, or perhaps with the next level of management. In some cases the employee would go on to the second level of management before the shop steward was involved. In some cases it was intended that the shop steward would only be involved if the employee so wished. At the other extreme it was accepted that the steward would make the first approach to management on behalf of the employee. In some cases the steward would go first not to the supervisor but to whichever representative of management he felt would be most likely to solve the problem quickly. Where written procedures existed it was rare indeed for the prescribed procedure to be consistently or universally followed. In particular, a provision precluding any form of shop steward involvement at the first stage of procedure, that is in the initial approach to the employee's immediate superior, was often disregarded.

50 Important factors affecting the early handling of grievances are the attitudes of the employee, his supervisor and the shop steward concerned. For example, if the action of a supervisor upsets an employee, say in the allocation of work, his instinctive reaction may be to go straight to the supervisor to complain. But a grievance may formulate only gradually in the employee's mind. He may nurse it for days, even weeks, during which time he may mention it to a colleague. The colleague may advise him to talk to his shop steward. The shop steward may advise him to go to his supervisor. On the other hand the steward may decide to take the matter up himself, not necessarily because he likes to keep business in his own hands; he may recognise a potential source of trouble or the member may be nervous and disinclined to act on his own. The employee may decide that a particular problem would best be settled by going direct to the pay office, the work study engineer or the personnel officer. He may do so not being absolutely certain who, for his particular problem, his immediate boss is. An older employee may not fully accept his immediate boss, for example because he is a recent appointment, and may consider himself to be in special relationship with the managing director. The managing director himself may have encouraged an 'open door' policy while also subscribing to the principle of grievance resolution 'up the line' – a frequent cause of confusion as well as irritation to lower levels of management.

51 A supervisor's response to an employee coming to him with a grievance is conditioned both by his ability to settle the matter himself and by his readiness to settle it. These can be considered separately though clearly they inter-act upon each other. The supervisor's ability to settle a matter himself depends on the authority allowed or delegated to him by more senior management and the nature of the grievance. If the action giving rise to the complaint lies within his field of responsibility, for example the allocation of overtime, and if his own boss expects and encourages him to deal with day-to-day problems himself, he is likely to try to settle the grievance. If however there is doubt about the area in which he may make his own decisions and his boss supervises his actions closely, he is likely to react less positively and the grievance is more likely to be taken further. If the grievance concerns terms and conditions of employment, for example if it impinges upon a plant-, company-, or even industry-wide payment or grading scheme, the supervisor's involvement is a matter of degree. Does he refer the employee to the specialist who can deal with the problem and opt out altogether, or does he take the matter up himself, and if so does he take part in subsequent discussions? Similarly if the grievance concerns physical conditions, for example a complaint about ventilation, he has the choice of reporting the matter himself, which may give him an implied responsibility for checking that the complaint is dealt with, or of referring the employee to the responsible department, thus divesting himself of responsibility for the outcome.

52   Much therefore depends on how the supervisor or manager sees his job and how his superiors see it, which in turn influence the amount of responsibility he is able or prepared to take. Some supervisors recognise that their status and authority in the eyes of their workgroups depend not only on their technical skills but also on their readiness to deal with any personal problems, including grievances, that may come up. If they cannot solve a grievance themselves they make sure that they remain involved. Other supervisors see or find themselves in a more limited role and keep their involvement in grievance handling to a minimum. If the work-group is represented by an active shop steward supervisors may be only too glad to push what they regard as 'personnel' or 'industrial relations' problems on to the personnel or industrial relations department as quickly as possible.

53   Under a piecework payment system the supervisor is likely to find himself, whether he likes it or not, in the thick of industrial relations. In that situation there is a direct relationship between an employee's work-load, his pace of work and what he earns. His interests and those of the supervisor, concerned with meeting production targets, are both involved in continual shopfloor decisions about processing the work. Decisions over waiting time, piecework prices, the timing of new jobs and so forth bring the supervisor, the steward and the employee concerned into frequent contact, with or without the rate-fixer or other specialist whose job it is to take account of the wider implications of the point at issue. Even where the supervisor ought, in the interests of preserving the integrity of the payment system, to insist on a fuller and wider investigation of the problem at a higher level in procedure, he may be tempted in his own immediate short-term interests to negotiate an *ad hoc* settlement of a grievance. Senior managers, similarly influenced by short-term cost and market considerations, may also tacitly countenance such discretionary action by the supervisor. Or they may simply be unaware of what is going on.

54   Where piecework systems are replaced by a time-rate payment system the supervisor's role changes considerably. He no longer has such a direct influence on the take home pay of his subordinates and in consequence his importance may be diminished in their eyes. Yet upon the supervisor still largely depends the level of productivity achieved by the work-group. He must still obtain from them the standards of performance necessary to meet production targets.

55 In a change from piecework to a different pay system the supervisor has to draw on different managerial skills. The exercise of discipline, for example, assumes a new significance. Unless steps are taken to meet the new situation, for example through appropriate training, his authority and effectiveness are likely to be impaired, and also therefore his ability to settle at or near the point of origin such grievances as are within his scope.

56 A supervisor's ability and readiness to solve or attempt to solve a grievance may be affected by whether he is approached in the first place by the employee alone, by the employee and steward together, or by the steward alone. If the employee approaches him unaccompanied, the supervisor may respond more confidently than if he comes with the steward. If the steward is there, or if the steward comes alone, the supervisor may well take up a defensive position which could inhibit a speedy solution. Premature involvement of the union may create in him the feeling that the problem is already outside his sphere of responsibility, or that it will soon move there, thus reducing his interest in trying to solve it himself. Though in some situations the steward may deliberately seek to make the first approach to management on behalf of the employee, this is by no means always the case. In one company the stewards said that when employees came to them with a grievance they encouraged them to follow procedure, which required them to go first to the supervisor. They argued that if management could solve the problem it saved them trouble and enabled them to concentrate on more important matters. It also absolved them from the charge of breaching procedure.

57 If an employee goes first to the steward and asks him to take up a grievance on his behalf, it may be difficult for the steward to refuse, even though he may prefer for the reasons just given to observe procedure. If he refuses, he risks losing face with a member. Stewards are often, therefore, glad of management's support in insisting on procedure being followed in this respect.

58 In some cases it was accepted practice for the union to make the approach first to management on behalf of the employee, for example in the printing industry. Generally, however, the normal practice — at any rate in theory — was for the individual to make his own first approach and this was widely reflected in written procedures. Here is an example from a chemical company:

> 'If an employee wishes to make a complaint he should approach
> his supervisor before reporting to his shop steward. If no
> satisfactory agreement can be reached he should either see his manager
> or inform his shop steward who will try to reach a settlement with
> the supervisor, or if necessary, take the matter to higher authority'.

This example reflects in writing the uncertainty which commonly exists as to what happens after failure to resolve at the first level of management. The language setting out the procedure is also more tentative than that used, for example, in the following extract from an engineering company's procedure, jointly agreed by management and the unions concerned:

'In the event of a grievance arising in matters directly affecting work or conditions of work the employee concerned will take the matter up with his supervisor. At this stage the grievance concerns only the individual and it is expected that normally it will be resolved at this level'.

59 In the agreement just quoted a grievance of any type affecting work or conditions of work is heard first by the supervisor, which is important for his relationship with his workgroup. If the grievance is not settled by the supervisor there is special provision for grievances affecting job grading or piecework application, which are referred to the work study department. If they are not resolved there, they are brought back to line management, stage two in the procedure involving the head of department. Similar arrangements were found in other companies.

60 In some organisations procedures for handling grievances in particular areas, for example those arising from the application of a productivity scheme or a job evaluation scheme, had a quite separate existence from the general grievance/disputes procedure. In one case the grievance procedure was described as dealing only with 'residual problems', there being special arrangements for dealing with issues arising from the ordering and cancelling of overtime, the allocation of work and so forth. Procedural differentiation to that extent may be thought to be excessive. There are, however, many advantages to both management and unions in recognising that different issues call for different treatment. Many redundancy agreements, for example, contain special procedural provisions including a special appeals procedure and grievances about job grading and piecework application are often dealt with in a purpose-built procedure. The degree of differentiation desirable depends on volume of business and any improvements in speed, efficacy and acceptability which can be looked for from specialised procedures.

61 Different considerations arise when a grievance affects a group of employees. A group needs a spokesman and, in a unionised establishment, the job will normally fall naturally to a union representative. In the case of a grievance affecting a group of employees responsible to the same supervisor, the steward may approach the supervisor. In the case of a grievance affecting employees in more than one department, the first approach will probably be to a member of middle or senior management whose span of control extends to all the employees concerned, which may raise some problems in defining responsibilities. Many procedures, however, take no account at all of collective issues, having been constructed entirely round the handling of individual grievances, on the apparent assumption that such collective issues as do arise will be dealt with at the appropriate level. In only half of the domestic procedures analysed was there provision for a collective issue to be referred in the first instance to a stage in procedure beyond the first stage.

62 From the point of view of a steward or convenor, the 'appropriate level' will be the level at which he considers he can most effectively negotiate and obtain speedy satisfaction for his members. Senior managers may disagree with the union representatives on what the appropriate level is, but through lack of clarity in the definition of responsibilities and through unwillingness to delegate responsibility they may find themselves in a weak position to challenge an overcentralised and top-heavy arrangement that has become established by custom and practice. In these situations the personnel department often bears a heavy burden in dealing with union representations on matters which could have been cleared with line management.

63 Many written procedures provide for a joint management-union committee as a stage in procedure. Most of the committees whose operation was examined in field inquiries took the form of a standing body, made up of equal numbers of management and trade union representatives, which met at regular intervals. In one company with particularly sophisticated procedural arrangements there were two special joint dispute committees — in addition to a joint negotiating committee and a works committee. One of the disputes committees dealt exclusively with issues involving 'piece time values' and consisted of a member of line management, members of the work study and personnel departments and trade union representatives. The second, known as the joint appeals committee, was made up of three management and three union members and dealt with all other issues that had come up through procedure.

64 Where a grievance procedure includes collective issues within its scope grievance handling readily merges into negotiation on claims and the existence as a stage in procedure of a joint body which is also the established negotiating body provides an integrated agency for resolving the matters at issue. Some aspects of the functioning of such bodies were considered in the previous chapter where it was noted that the distinction between negotiation and consultation was sometimes expressed through separate systems of representation for the two purposes. Such a dual system can cause particular problems in the handling of individual grievances.

65 In several large organisations in the public sector, for example, employee representation for trade union purposes was separate from employee representation on the formal joint committees at establishment level. It was a requirement that representatives on these committees should be members of unions recognised at national level, but they were not necessarily shop stewards. In one undertaking an employee's official representative in the grievance procedure was his committee representative. Yet the latter might well not be a member of his own union, let alone his shop steward. In practice he would turn to his shop steward, whom management might or might not acknowledge as his representative. Consequently a good deal of vagueness surrounded representation in the early handling of grievances. An unnecessarily high number of grievances had to go for resolution to the final stage in domestic procedure because that was the first stage at which there would be representatives of his own union. In another undertaking it was actually acknowledged in a written agreement that there were two distinct channels for processing a grievance to the local committee which constituted the final stage in domestic procedure, one through the 'official' representative, the other through the trade union organisation.

66 Some grievance procedures embody time limits for each stage. An employee or group of employees with a grievance wants that grievance settled as soon as possible. They may well regard it as a great deal more important than anything else which the manager to whom they present it may currently have on his plate. The manager for his part needs time to gather the facts, consult with other managers and consider what action to take, all of which must be fitted in with his other duties. The idea behind a time limit is that it gives the manager an opportunity to consider the problem whilst also committing him to providing an answer within a fixed period of time. This temporarily relaxes the pressure from the employee or shop steward who knows that if a satisfactory answer has not been provided at the end of the time limit, the issue can be taken to the next stage in procedure.

67 There were many opinions on the usefulness or otherwise of time limits. The management of one company took the view that it was the job of the unions to ensure that grievances were processed quickly and had refused to include time limits in a recognition and procedure agreement they had just signed with a white-collar union. Another company had agreed to a clause which stated that 'management undertakes to deal promptly with all questions arising at each stage in the procedure' but had likewise been unwilling to tie itself down to specific time limits. One management went so far as to say that they considered time limits to be 'very dangerous' as they would undermine mutual trust. A number of both management and union representatives expressed concern over the loss of flexibility which time limits could induce. It was pointed out that they sometimes had the effect of forcing an issue through procedure without allowing sufficient time for it to be dealt with properly at the lower levels, where it might have been solved. On the other hand many union representatives felt that it was helpful to be able to point to an agreed time limit. Some managers complained that unions wanted time limits, but it was often difficult to get hold of union officials to take part in meetings within the prescribed period. Some union representatives on the other hand complained that management, by taking advantage of the full time allowed, needlessly delayed resolution of an issue. Many managers found time limits to be a useful discipline. In one company, where it was claimed that the time limits were 'always observed and usually beaten', it was said that they were particularly useful to the personnel department in monitoring the operation of procedure.

68 The usual practice is to allow progressively longer time limits between stages as an issue passes up through procedure. At domestic level, for example, they may range from 24 hours to five days, longer in the external stages. Time limits alone will not ensure the expeditious handling of grievances but they serve a useful purpose in establishing agreed standards of what is thought to be reasonable. In external stages when the initiative for resolving an issue passes to some extent out of the hands of the parties directly concerned they provide a useful reassurance against fears of indefinite delay. Most of the doubts and criticisms of time limits can be met if there is a proviso which allows them to be extended by mutual agreement.

69 When an issue passes to a higher stage in procedure a certain amount of documentation is necessary for the benefit of those who are not familiar with the claims of the parties and the supporting evidence. At domestic level the extent to which records of grievances were kept varied widely. In some establishments the completion of grievance records was a required drill for line management, in some cases on specially designed grievance record forms. In others only the personnel department kept any records. In others there was no documentation of any kind, except when an issue was referred to external procedure.

70 Grievance records serve several useful purposes. If there is failure to agree at any stage, a written record clarifies the facts and the contentions of the parties and is helpful to those involved in the next stage in procedure. If the record is agreed by both parties – commonly completed by the manager concerned and counter-signed by the employee or union representative – it is even more valuable. Grievance record forms can help the personal department to keep in touch with the progress of unresolved grievances. The records are useful for analysing the causes of grievances. Analysis may also show where and why delays in procedure most frequently occur. When a settlement has been reached, a written and agreed statement helps to ensure that there are no misunderstandings. In the absence of an agreed statement the parties may find that they have different versions of the terms of the settlement. A written statement is also useful for communicating the outcome.

71 Establishments which had introduced a system which required line management to keep records of grievances had not found it easy to keep the system going. For supervisors in particular, who handle most individual grievances, it was an extra, irksome administrative chore and the records system did not operate effectively at supervisor level. One or two companies where the records system operated from departmental manager level reported more favourably.

72 Some companies, concerned about the operation of the grievance and disputes procedures, introduce a records system for a limited period, for example three or six months, during which time all levels of management are required to keep records. This enables the company to identify problem areas and introduce reforms. Where a permanent records system is desired, it may be more realistic to operate it only beyond the initial level in procedure.

73 Many grievance procedures are purely domestic being concerned essentially with laying down a recognised method of bringing a grievance to attention and securing further consideration of the issue if it is not settled when first raised. This is normally achieved through a staged procedure of progressive reference to higher authority. Such a pattern presents special problems for small firms though the ideas of a recognised orderly method and provision for bringing more than a single judgement to bear can be successfully applied even in quite small firms.* Even in large organisations, however, where there is no difficulty in providing for domestic consideration of an unresolved issue at a point sufficiently detached from its origin, the issue may remain unresolved.

74 The final stage of domestic procedure may be the end of the road for both small and large firms but both may have recourse to outside help through the external stages of an industry-wide procedure. Of the industry procedures studied 98 per cent contained provisions for resolving disputes at industry level, the large majority being incorporated in jointly-negotiated

*CIR Report No 69: 'Small Firms and the Code of Industrial Relations Practice'.

agreements. 78 per cent of the agreements also contained provisions for dispute resolution at domestic level and 44 per cent at intermediate level. The commonest provision for dispute resolution at industry level was some form of joint disputes committee but 17 per cent of the agreements provided for a joint arbitration body drawn from within the industry with the power to make an award.

75 Both management and unions normally prefer to settle at domestic level rather than commit an issue to external procedures. For both the parties immediately concerned resort to external procedure means to some extent surrendering their control over the outcome and both may wish to avoid the magnification of the issue and the delay which may result. Thus, although attitudes on both sides may be hardening, extra efforts to resolve the issue by informal methods are likely to be made. This preference for domestic settlements was found not only in relation to industry-wide procedures but also in relation to company-level procedures in the case of multi-location undertakings.

76 Officials of trade unions and employer bodies sometimes become involved informally in disputes or potential disputes at domestic level when there is no provision for it in an agreement. They may intervene only at a point when failure to agree appears inevitable, and be restricted to sorting out the exact area of disagreement and advising on the first stage of external procedure. On the other hand, they may come in at a point where their advice or help may be instrumental in preventing the issue from going beyond domestic level.

77 Such involvement may not always, however, be necessary. In one engineering company it was stressed that a full-time union official would be introduced at Works Conference and not before. Similarly, in another engineering company it was said to be a matter of pride on the part of the shop stewards negotiating committee not to involve their officials at all. The works committee was the last stage in domestic procedure. If there was failure to agree there, procedure was described as 'effectively exhausted', even though the company was federated. In both these companies there was well developed domestic machinery, an active personnel function and a commitment on both sides to domestic control of industrial relations issues.

78 All the industries whose procedures were investigated recognised the importance of containing issues at domestic level wherever possible but some took more positive steps than others to try to achieve this end. Some industries attached particular importance to settlements being reached in the locality where the dispute had occurred, even after failure to agree at domestic level. For example, the joint industrial council of the cable-making industry will send representatives to a plant if it is considered that there is a chance of achieving an *ad hoc* settlement. In the municipal transport industry the 'emergency committee' of the national joint industrial council goes to the actual location of a dispute to attempt to solve it.

79   In the paper and board making industry it was understood that unresolved issues at plant level should not pass into the external procedure if they related only to that plant on the argument that use of the industry procedure should be confined to issues of industry-wide significance. It might be considered that such a practice restricts the opportunity of achieving a peaceful settlement but it is argued that if the parties know that failure to agree at domestic level is the end of the line, they are more likely to settle at that level. In other words, the availability of an external procedure may weaken the parties' resolve to settle local issues locally.

80   In the engineering industry, the termination of the national procedure agreement for manual workers at the end of 1971 meant that, after failure to agree at local level, procedure was exhausted. Many employers said that the termination of the agreement had induced a greater determination to settle locally though they recognised a need for an industry-wide agreement to deal with issues affecting the whole industry.

81   A distinction between local and national issues is embodied in the agreement made in 1973 between the EEF and the white-collar unions APEX, ACTSS and MATSA, which specifies that the following matters require national consideration:

   The amount of holiday entitlement

   The length of the working week

   The payment for overtime or shift working

   The interpretation or implementation of national agreements or nationally agreed guideline documents

   The recognition of a union for a group of employees or an employee and issues related to recognition questions.

If an issue concerning any of these matters is not resolved at the first stage in the external procedure, that is at a works conference, it passes straight to national level. Any other issue not resolved at works conference is referred to a Local Conference, and this is the last stage in procedure, unless there is mutual agreement to refer salary matters of industry-wide significance to national level.

82   The recognition of the growing importance of negotiations at company and factory level and the Donovan Commission recommendations

to develop institutions and procedures which would acknowledge and more effectively discharge that responsibility is matched by a similar trend in the evolution of disputes procedures. The procedure for dealing with grievances and the resolution of disputes arising from them has always been considered to be essentially a subject for local treatment in the first instance and nationally negotiated disputes procedures generally outlined the structure and principles of domestic procedures. But such provisions in national agreements inevitably appeared merely as the initial stages of a national procedure. Increasingly it has been recognised that more is needed than reliance on the provisions relating to the domestic stage in a nationally negotiated procedure agreement. Domestic procedures have to take almost the whole load of dealing with grievances and disputes and need to be worked out in detail to suit the local circumstances and conditions giving rise to that business.

83 Greater recognition of the importance of developing adequate domestic grievance and disputes procedures makes greater demands of the personnel function. This is not just a matter of appointing specialist staff though a specialised personnel department plays a major part in the development and operation of procedures and in analysing the information which they generate. Procedures for dealing with grievances and disputes are integral to the whole way in which an enterprise is managed. They directly affect line management at all levels. A good understanding of such procedures is needed by all managers and account should be taken of this requirement in management training programmes.

84 Increasing attention to domestic procedures by companies and establishments has been matched by changes of policy and in the services provided at national level. National agreements which distinguish local from national issues and exclude purely local issues from entering all but the first external stage emphasise the need for adequate domestic procedures and are in harmony with company agreements which provide for final resolution of local issues at domestic level. Employers' associations and trade unions provide advice on the development of domestic procedures and give informal assistance to parties to enable them to reach local settlements. Containment of disputes at domestic level does not exclude third party assistance; some of the forms which this takes and the services available to parties are considered in Chapter 6.

85 To many people 'the procedure' means the jointly agreed grievance and disputes procedure. It is of course a very important feature arising from a negotiating relationship but it is only one area for the procedural

regulation of the relations of the parties. The more successful the parties are in developing a whole range of jointly agreed procedures for the handling of business in which they both have an interest, the less strain is likely to be placed on the grievance and disputes procedure. Procedures in some of these other areas are considered in the two following chapters.

4 Disciplinary procedures

86 A disciplinary procedure is in many ways the converse of a grievance procedure. In a grievance procedure an employee is concerned with something unsatisfactory in the employer's performance or at least within the employer's power to alter; in a disciplinary procedure the employer is concerned with something unsatisfactory in the employee's performance. Where action on these matters is contained within a procedure it may develop in both cases through a process of discussions, warnings and sanctions. Action in a grievance procedure is initiated by the employee; disciplinary action is initiated by the employer. The development of both grievance and disciplinary procedures reflects changes in the relative powers of employers and employees and in the social and political context within which they are exercised.

87 Discipline at work is related to the general context of working conditions. The two main instruments for restraining the strong and in many respects arbitrary powers of employers to impose harsh working conditions in the period following the Industrial Revolution have been the law and the trade unions. The intervention of the law has been mainly through general measures to ameliorate working conditions on the lines of the Factories Acts and minimum wage legislation and it is only in recent years that legislation has directly entered the disciplinary sphere by providing remedies against unfair dimissals. Legal remedies are available to all. Trade union help is available only in those areas where employees are effectively organised but in those areas unions play a much more influential role than the law both in regulating working conditions and by the protection they offer to their members against arbitrary or unjustified disciplinary action. This is achieved both through representations in individual cases and by agreeing with employers' procedures for the exercise of disciplinary powers.

88 The use of the word 'unfair' in the legislation on dismissals gives an interesting pointer to the criteria and the forces which sustain a successful disciplinary policy. Fairness will reflect the general sentiment of fellow workers. They often have a very powerful interest in seeing that discipline is maintained. This may arise from a shared common interest in questions of safety or in the effect on the pay packet of operations dependent on team-work or it may merely reflect a general sentiment of irritation by the majority against an individual who does not conform to the conditions which they are prepared to accept as reasonable. Fairness also requires

consistency of treatment. For this purpose there must be clearly recognised rules and standards of work behaviour. The interests of employers and employees are brought together and disciplinary problems reduced when the rules which employees are required to keep and the standards they are expected to maintain are clearly known and generally accepted.

89   A common means of attempting to make rules known is through employee handbooks and works rule books. Many of these documents were studied during the inquiries. They varied widely in content. Rules relating to attendance and absence were among the most common features. Other examples were use of safety equipment, smoking in prohibited areas, consumption of alcohol on the premises and use of the company's telephone for personal calls. The technology or function of the organisation may call for special rules. The employee handbook of a tobacco company had rules relating to employees having in their possession the company's own brand of cigarette. In the lengthy Railway Operations Rule Book of London Transport safety regulations constituted a substantial proportion of the rules. In food and pharmaceutical companies rules relating to personal hygiene were a common feature.

90   Written rules provide an adducible source of authority, though they may not be used so much in the exercise of discipline as in appeals. When a manager confronts an employee with a breach of discipline it is unusual for him to wave the rule book at him. Nor does the employee usually question the manager's right to discipline him. The employee may, however, question the justification of the case the manager is making against him and appeal against the action taken. Judicial consideration of an appeal calls for the identification of authority and the presentation of evidence. The advantage in such circumstances of written over unwritten rules is apparent.

91   But it is the educative and preventive rather than the judicial use of written rules which is most valuable. The least satisfactory way of discovering that a rule exists is by breaking it. There is less chance of that happening if, upon appointment, a new employee is provided with a set of written rules since at the outset he can familiarize himself with what is expected of him. Some employers obtain a signed statement from the employee to the effect that he has received and read the rules and undertakes to abide by them. While this may be a useful precaution, it is not as valuable as a verbal explanation of the rules, particularly the more important ones, during the new employee's induction.

92   Written rules are very desirable for subjects which lend themselves to clear-cut formulations of general application. But the maintenance of good

discipline and the avoidance of the need for disciplinary action are subjects which far transcend what can be looked for from compliance with a written code. The important subject of 'discipline avoidance' is mentioned later in this chapter after considering some features of the operation of disciplinary systems.

93   The term 'offence', although in many cases hardly the natural or appropriate language, is nevertheless used here for the purpose of examining the operation of procedures. It is used broadly to cover any breach of rules and any failure to meet required standards, from a minor misdemeanour to a major contravention of the rules, which is subject to formal disciplinary action.

94   Within a company and between one company and another the gravity of an offence varies according to a number of factors. People's lives depend on the quality of motor tyres. They do not normally depend on the quality of paper bags. Faulty workmanship is therefore likely to be regarded as more serious in a tyre-manufacturing company than in a company making paper bags. In an explosives factory smoking in a prohibited area may entail summary dismissal. In a factory where there is no direct risk to life but the rule is important, for example in a food factory, it may incur a sanction short of dismissal for a first offence. Even within the same factory or office location different criteria may be applied. For example lateness may be viewed more seriously in situations where the function of the workgroup depends on close team work than in situations where the members of the group can work independently. A higher premium may be placed upon punctuality in manual worker departments than in the offices. Even between managers and supervisors in charge of similar operations, there will be differences in approach. The use of the ultimate sanction of dismissal may be affected by the state of the labour market.

95   These examples are a reminder of the local and often arbitrary nature of industrial discipline. Discipline may be less arbitrarily exercised if some codification of offences exists.

96   A distinction can be drawn between offences which are held to warrant summary dismissal and those which call — initially at any rate — for disciplinary action short of dismissal. Offences warranting summary dismissal are commonly termed 'gross misconduct'. Some companies specify in their contracts of employment, or in their published rules, or in the disciplinary procedure (or in all three) which offences are regarded as constituting gross misconduct carrying a liability to incur the penalty of summary dismissal. Others simply refer to gross misconduct but do not specify which offences fall into this category. Others make no reference

at all to gross misconduct in documentary form. The managements of companies in which there is no documentary reference to gross misconduct, specific or otherwise, do not necessarily act in an arbitrary manner; there may well be well-established custom and practice. But specific reference leaves less room for doubt and makes for greater consistency.

97 Offences other than those warranting summary dismissal can conveniently be classified as 'minor' and 'serious', though these categories cannot be absolute. What may in the first instance be a relatively trivial misdemeanour, for example bad timekeeping, becomes increasingly serious with a persistent offender. What starts as a minor offence may ultimately warrant dismissal. There can be no clear-cut division between one category and another. Some employers do identify, however, certain 'first offences' which are not serious enough to warrant dismissal but which, if committed a second time, would be.

98 In pursuing the analysis of the disciplinary process it is convenient to borrow more terminology from a loose analogy with judicial proceedings. When the supervisor (or manager) decides on the evidence available that formal disciplinary action is required and prepares for a disciplinary interview he normally acts as both prosecutor and judge. However thoroughly he may prepare for the interview – checking the facts, examining the employee's record card, establishing whether there is any precedent for the action he proposes to take – it is impossible for him to obtain the full picture without talking to the employee himself. The employee for his part may have wind of impending action, but until he is confronted with a charge and the evidence in support of it he cannot properly prepare a defence. Yet the normal practice is to have a single disciplinary interview, at which the supervisor tells the employee what he is charged with, presents the evidence, hears the employee's case and delivers a judgement – but not necessarily in that order.

99 The temptation to 'sentence' the employee in advance is strong. Indeed it is significant that most disciplinary procedures are constructed on the assumption that the outcome of the disciplinary interview is a foregone conclusion. Thus there is a tendency for the supervisor to state early in the interview what disciplinary action he is proposing to take, leaving the employee or his representative to respond not to a charge and the evidence in support of it but to a judgement. Mitigating circumstances may well come out during the interview which cause the supervisor to alter his view of the case. His authority is more easily and firmly maintained if he refrains from stating his view and more particularly the action he proposes to take until he has heard and considered the representations of the employee or his representative. If he commits himself to a judgement at the

outset, he runs the risk of either appearing to disregard the evidence if he maintains his position or of losing face through appearing to backtrack or through being reversed on appeal.

100   A hearing before sentence is not only good tactics for the supervisor, but more importantly it is likely to result in greater justice, greater respect for the disciplinary system and fewer problems for those who have to consider appeals. In some cases a further interview or an adjournment may be desirable to see that representations are properly considered. In all cases those conducting disciplinary interviews should be trained to observe the proper sequence of events required to uphold the principle.

101   The following quotation comes from the disciplinary procedure embodied in a plant agreement between an employer and three unions in a company in the engineering industry. The section of the disciplinary procedure dealing with lateness and absenteeism starts with a rule stating that employees must start work on time and continue to work through until the end of the shift. Offences are then defined: 'Two days unauthorised absence in any four week period or less' and 'Lateness in excess of the (mutually-agreed) three-minute allowance on more than one occasion in any one week'. Finally the disciplinary measures which will be applied are listed:

First occasion: caution by the unit manager, to be recorded in departmental records.

Second occasion: warning by unit manager in presence of shop steward and a written warning sent to the offender by the personnel manager.

Third occasion: suspension of two days without pay by the unit manager in presence of shop steward.

Fourth occasion: dismissal by unit manager in presence of senior shop steward'.

Following this there is a provision to the effect that all warnings under the procedure will be deleted from the records after eight working weeks in which there has been no more than one instance of unauthorised lateness or absenteeism.

102   This example is of interest in a number of respects:
   (a) The procedure differentiates clearly between rules, offences and disciplinary measures (or sanctions)
   (b) It shows that the treatment to be accorded to certain minor offences, in this case lateness and absenteeism, may be quantified and agreed with the unions

(c) It shows how repetition of the same offence may incur sanctions of increasing severity

(d) It provides for the sanctions most commonly used: warnings of one kind or another, suspension without pay and dismissal. (Less common are fines, deductions, transfer and demotion)

(e) It distinguishes between a formal verbal warning and the more serious written warning

(f) It provides for the registering of sanctions of an admonitory nature. The first verbal warning is noted in the records. The second, written warning is also registered through the copy of the letter on the employee's file

(g) There is a 'clean slate' provision which ensures that if an employee reforms after receiving verbal or written warnings the offences are not indefinitely held against him.

103 In the above procedure suspension without pay is used as a sanction. Suspension may, however, be used as a temporary holding measure pending investigation of an alleged offence of a serious nature. One practice in such cases is to suspend without pay on the argument that should investigation confirm a case for summary dismissal the penalty should apply from the time of the occurrence of the offence while if the case is not established payment for the period of suspension can then be made. Other firms argue that suspension with pay better supports belief in the reality of the process of investigation and that the appropriate time from which the penalty should apply is after the facts have been established and a decision reached. In one company the decision to dismiss an employee for gross misconduct could not be taken until 24 hours after the identification of the supposed offence. For that period the employee was suspended with pay pending investigation of the facts. In some situations, for example on a night shift, it may be appropriate to send a man home until more senior management can be consulted and the facts investigated properly.

104 Where suspension without pay was used as a sanction the period of suspension rarely exceeded five days. In most of the establishments where it was used, it was not regarded as a particularly satisfactory measure, its main value being seen as an alternative to dismissal. For example, it could be used as a compromise in a case normally warranting dismissal where mitigating circumstances had been established but a reprimand would have been an inadequate measure.

105 An employer only has the right to suspend an employee without pay where:

(a) There are express or implied terms in the individual contract of employment allowing him to do so;

(b) The suspension is carried out in conformity with those terms;

(c) The grounds for which suspension can be used are specified.

There must either, therefore, be written contractual provision for it or it must be shown that the right to suspend is unmistakably established by custom and practice.

106 Following the provisions in the Industrial Relations Act 1971 giving protection to employees against unfair dismissal, there was a general move to raise the level of management with the authority to dismiss. The prospect of a case going to an Industrial Tribunal increased the importance accorded by management to dismissal decisions. In the procedure quoted, which was drawn up with the Act in mind, a 'unit manager' is two levels removed from the work-group. Untypically, in that company supervisors are not responsible for administering even the mildest sanction. The more usual practice was for first line supervisors to issue formal warnings. In some cases they could also suspend without pay. Only in one company did the supervisor have the authority to dismiss, and then only after consulting his superior.

107 The decision to dismiss is an extremely serious one and should never be taken lightly irrespective of the legal remedies now available to employees. It is appropriate therefore, that such a decision should be taken by a senior level of management. This is not incompatible with the need to maintain the authority and status of first-line supervisors but a decision merely to upgrade authority for dismissal decisions could undermine the position of supervisors unless care is taken to see that they have an appropriate role in the procedural steps preceding a final decision. This, of course, is only one item in the general need for careful definition of the duties and powers of supervisors.

108 Arrangements for appeal against disciplinary action took various forms. In some organisations the disciplinary procedure included a special appeals procedure for all cases; in others there were special provisions for appeals against dismissal, all other appeals against disciplinary action being processed through the normal grievance procedure; in others it was intended that appeals of any kind should be processed through the normal grievance procedure; and in some there were no regular identifiable arrangements.

109 It is desirable that an appeal system should provide for the case to be reviewed by an authority other than that which has administered the sanction. An appeal may be against a sanction administered by the employee's own superior, who is normally the first stage in the grievance procedure. On that score, therefore, the normal grievance procedure does not appear to be a satisfactory medium of appeal – though it does give the manager or supervisor concerned an opportunity to change his mind. A further argument against the use of the grievance procedure is that it normally has provision for at least three, sometimes four or five, domestic stages, which is clearly inappropriate for an appeal against dismissal and indeed for appealing against action short of dismissal.

110 There are strong arguments in favour of a special appeals procedure, quite separate from the normal grievance procedure. If the circumstances of an offence have been thoroughly investigated and the disciplinary interview conducted along the judicial lines discussed earlier, only one, possibly two, appeal stages should be necessary at domestic level, though some of the procedures investigated had three.

111 At the time a formal sanction is administered the employee should be informed of his right to appeal and of the procedure to be followed. Many organisations specify a time limit within which an appeal must be lodged, either 24 or 48 hours being the most common. Some also specify a further limit within which the appeal must be heard. The speed with which appeals are heard is clearly more important in the case of sanctions affecting the pocket or livelihood of the employee than of those which are purely admonitory in nature.

112 An appeal against disciplinary action is essentially a domestic affair without the wider implications which may, for example, attend the processing of some grievances which concern the application of industry-wide agreements. Although some disciplinary cases can give rise to disputes involving the external stages of industry-wide procedures appeals against disciplinary action can normally be regarded as purely local matters. This does not, however, preclude the use of appeals machinery outside the establishment, for example in the form of independent arbitration. Indeed, an appeal against disciplinary action is particularly suitable for the quasi-judicial process of arbitration. There are practical advantages in holding the hearing in the locality of the establishment, though not necessarily on the premises. Witnesses, for example, are readily available. The further removed the hearing is from the establishment, both physically and psychologically, the harder it may be to achieve a quick and satisfactory solution. In one public sector industry which had provisions for independent arbitration at industry level, it was reported that up to 18 months might elapse before an appeal was finally disposed of.

113 In the industry-wide procedures analysed which covered disciplinary matters, provision for appeal at industry level was less common than appeal at domestic level only. A few procedures provided for appeal at both domestic and industry level. The recent agreement between the EEF and the white collar unions already quoted (para 81) includes an external stage on a local basis by providing that an appeal may be taken to a Local Conference as the final stage in the procedure. Officials of employers' associations and trade unions often give valuable assistance to their members by informal advice on the handling at domestic level of appeals in disciplinary cases. This is useful not only where there is no formal external procedure but also for avoiding the magnification of issues by invoking external procedures for essentially domestic matters.

114 There is now a statutory means of appeal against unfair dismissal. This has the great advantage of being universally available. Where effective voluntary procedures exist however they are a much more satisfactory method for dealing with disciplinary matters. They are not confined to dismissal cases, they cover the constitution and operation of the disciplinary system, they can be suitably flexible and their existence is an indication of a generally sound system for the conduct of industrial relations. In unfair dismissal cases industrial tribunals pay attention to agreed arrangements for dealing with cases. Their decisions have in turn established points of principle and good practice which have influenced voluntary procedures.

115 In disciplinary procedures, as in other types of procedure concerned with the interests and treatment of employees, there has been a historical development from sole management responsibility for the formulation and operation of the procedure to a position where some aspects of that responsibility are shared with representatives of the employees. Again, as with other procedures, within a general trend there is a wide variety of practice. In very large numbers of places of employment all procedures, more or less consciously formulated, remain a sole management responsibility with varying degrees and forms of consultation to take account of the views of employees. But disciplinary matters have in general been regarded both by managements and unions as less suitable than other topics such as negotiation on terms and conditions of employment or the treatment of grievances for bringing within the ambit of jointly agreed procedures. A commonly held view is that the maintenance of discipline is a management concern and that a union's function in representing the interests of its members should not be compromised by association with the disciplinary system.

116 The difference of functions and responsibilities of management and unions invoked in support of that view is a matter of objective fact. It is possible, however, to distinguish between those aspects of the disciplinary function which must remain the separate responsibilities of management and unions and those aspects which can properly be made the subject of joint agreement.

117 From the inquiries which were carried out it appeared that trade unions only rarely participated in the formulation of the rules of an establishment. They might challenge a particular rule, seeking perhaps to have it modified or rescinded. They were in general unwilling to join with management in determining the rules. Managers equally were in general opposed to having rule-making made the subject of negotiation and joint determination, though some managers saw advantage in inviting union comment on a consultative basis when drawing up or revising works rules. Similarly there is little joint management–union agreement upon what constitutes an offence. Union representations on behalf of a member may however result in mitigating the sanction applied and result in downgrading the offence through the effect of the precedent established.

118 It is more common to find union representatives involved in the procedures for the exercise of discipline than sharing in the formulation of the disciplinary code. They may be involved in three ways:

(a) helping to enforce rules and standards

(b) as the representative of an employee who is being disciplined

(c) on joint employer-union panels or similar bodies whose task it is to investigate alleged offences and impose disciplinary measures.

119 Safety provides perhaps the best example of an area in which unions most readily co-operate with management in the enforcement of rules. Co-operation over rule enforcement in other areas may lead to confusion over respective roles. Managers who take the view that it is reasonable to expect union co-operation are in fact asking representatives to carry out a managerial function, and this may diminish the effectiveness with which they perform their representative role. 'Whose side are you on?' their members may ask. For their part, supervision, having initially welcomed the prospect of union support, may come to feel that the shop stewards are taking over. In certain sections of the printing industry trade union representatives actually had taken over what is normally the supervisor's job in handling minor disciplinary problems. If an employee was keeping bad time, for example, the supervisor would not himself speak to the offender but ask the union representative to do it for him.

120 In representing an employee who is being disciplined, a shop steward is in effect acting as the employee's defence lawyer; this may be regarded as the union's conventional role in matters of discipline.

121 In some organisations union (or other) representatives attend formal disciplinary interviews only at the request of the employee concerned. In others their presence is a procedural requirement at any disciplinary interview. In others it is required only when more serious offences are being dealt with. In one procedure there was no provison for a steward to be present when a first warning was administered but his attendance was required at a second and any subsequent disciplinary interview.

122 There are advantages in the early involvement of representatives but the wishes of an employee who prefers a disciplinary interview to remain a confidential matter between himself and his superior need to be respected. One way of meeting both these objectives is for the supervisor or manager to call in the employee on his own, inform him of what he is charged with and the evidence in support of it and ask him if he would like his representative to be brought in. This is an arrangement which can readily be incorporated in written procedures and would accord well with the desirable practice of separating the charge from the sanction at a disciplinary interview.

123 If a shop steward considers that management's action or proposed action is justified, the job of representing the employee is not always easy. If a shop steward is brought in early on a disciplinary case, his job may be made very much easier. A number of the managers interviewed said that when they were contemplating disciplinary action they put the steward in the picture on an informal basis. Some claimed that the unions were 'usually with them' in the warning stages of the disciplinary procedure, but whenever a harsher penalty, such as suspension without pay or dismissal, was proposed, the representatives then moved firmly into the role of advocate, contesting the proposed action on whatever grounds they could muster.

124 Nowhere was management's right to initiate disciplinary action disputed. This included the establishments where trade union representatives acted as the mouthpiece of management in the early stages of dealing with minor offences. Where trade unions were strong management usually took care to establish the likely reaction of the union before taking any disciplinary action which would affect either the pocket or the livelihood of an employee. If they discovered by informal means that the union did not dissent from a proposal to dismiss an employee, they could act in the knowledge that the action would not give rise to a dispute. If on the other hand the union indicated opposition, or reserved its position, they had to take this into account before reaching a final decision.

125 In the docks the more serious disciplinary cases come under the National Dock Labour Scheme and are dealt with by joint management-union boards at national and port level. This is an unusual arrangement and is disliked by some port employers who complain that it is no longer possible to dismiss anyone at all. If union representatives are members of a disciplinary panel or similar body they appear to be sitting in judgement over their fellow employees, which provides a sharp contrast with their conventional representative role. Most managers and most trade union representatives were opposed to any sharing of decisions to impose disciplinary measures. Managers took the view that the exercise of discipline must be their responsibility and that trade union participation in disciplinary decisions would result in a deterioration in standards of work and behaviour; the unions would be placed in a position to veto any management proposal. For their part trade union representatives took the view that joint panels compromised their position in the eyes of their members and weakened their ability to represent their members effectively. They preferred to remain independent.

126 Nevertheless, there are situations where joint panels have worked to the satisfaction of both parties. In one company a joint panel dealt with the more serious disciplinary cases – none was referred to it unless the employee concerned had received at least two warnings. The panel consisted of the head of department concerned, the shop steward concerned, the convenor of the appropriate union and the personnel officer. In putting his case to the panel the employee could have with him another employee from his own department. Having put his case the employee was asked to withdraw while the panel discussed it. The head of department normally outlined the course he wished to adopt, which was accepted or disputed by the union representatives – usually the latter. Since the steward directly concerned was on the panel, in company with the convenor and the management representatives concerned, there was no question of the parties acting as neutrals. The panel could not impose a sanction unless it reached an agreed decision. If it could not, the case would be referred to the managing director – though this situation had never arisen.

127 The joint panel in another company consisted of the personnel manager, a line manager selected by the latter and a senior shop steward. Thus in this case the manager and steward directly involved were not on the panel. The panel again had to reach a unanimous decision and it was empowered to award either a reprimand, suspension or dismissal.

128 The availability of a number of possible sanctions provides the clue to an understanding of the way in which these joint panels operated. In form, union representatives were sitting in judgement over a member and fellow employee. In practice the deliberations of the panels took the form of negotiation. If it was established and agreed that an offence had been committed — and this was an important part of the job of the panel — the management members tended to suggest a more severe penalty than was necessary to allow a margin to bargain over. Thus the panels were institutionalising a collective bargaining process. The union representatives on the panels were not shedding their representative role and identifying with a managerial function.

129 In the first company the disciplinary panel had been introduced during the second world war. It was tried and tested and the managers and union representatives had grown up with it. It was not felt that discipline was 'slack' as a result of it. It was pointed out that a manager had to prepare a case very thoroughly before referring it to the panel as any flaws in it would quickly be detected.

130 In the second example the joint panel had been operating for about five years. It was one item in a complete overhaul of industrial relations in the company introduced following a joint management-union working party. So far as discipline was concerned, the unions pointed to the influence they could exert through formal channels and contrasted the new situation with the old, where foremen had had the right to hire and fire. Management was equally happy with the situation and claimed that discipline under the new procedure was tighter.

131 Of the industry-wide procedures analysed which made provision for disciplinary matters, about four-fifths specified the presence of union representatives at disciplinary interviews, but only a tiny minority made provision for union involvement on panels imposing disciplinary sanctions.

132 Union representation on an appellate body raises problems similar to those attending representation on a disciplinary panel. There is also a further problem if the union has participated in the work of a joint panel from whose decision the appeal is being heard. In that case there is a need for both management and union representatives to be dissociated from personal involvement in the earlier handling of the case.

133 It is evident that the question of whether discipline is best regarded as solely a management subject with the unions acting solely as advocates of their members' interests in response to management action or whether it offers scope for joint management-union working is not one question

but several. The answers to those questions suggested by the inquiries are as follows – subject always to the qualification that in industrial relations answers are not absolute and the inquiries also showed examples of successful working on different lines from those suggested here.

(a) The formulation and promulgation of disciplinary rules including any classification of offences and penalties is best carried out as a management responsibility and action but it is one on which consultation with unions, whether formal or informal, can be practised with advantage.

(b) The formulation of procedures setting out the course of action which will be followed in the consideration of disciplinary cases lends itself just as readily as a grievance procedure to joint agreement and there are advantages in having such jointly agreed procedures.

(c) The initiation and carrying through of disciplinary action is best undertaken as a management responsibility with union involvement in the role of advocacy of the interests of members.

(d) Periodic review of the operation of the disciplinary procedure can usefully be undertaken on a joint basis.

(e) At national level guidelines on the handling of disciplinary procedure can usefully be issued on a jointly agreed basis. Out of 51 disciplinary procedures at national level 36 were in the form of jointly negotiated agreements, 9 were guidelines from the employer organisation and 6 were jointly issued guidelines.

134 The advantages of written procedures in assisting clarity, consistency and general understanding have particular application to disciplinary matters. Written procedures help management to establish desired norms; employees like to know where they stand and to feel that they are subject to common, known rules and procedures; union officials and representatives are assisted in looking after their members' interests reasonably and effectively. All concerned in the disciplinary process benefit from the reduction in the arbitrary element which written procedures can contribute.

135 Dissatisfaction with the performance of an employee who clearly flouts the works rules is readily recognised as giving grounds for disciplinary action. Failure to maintain a proper standard of work, for example through carelessness or idleness is also seen as raising disciplinary issues. But failure to maintain a proper standard of work may only be an indication of limited capacity or inexperience rather than indiscipline and calls for quite different treatment. In many jobs, for example in clerical, technical and supervisory grades, the expected standards of performance require individual guidance from the employee's immediate superior. Regular and systematic appraisal interviews are one means of achieving this. They can help to check an employee's weaknesses and faults in good time and to avoid a development which might turn into a case for formal disciplinary action.

136 Appraisal schemes, job descriptions, recruitment and selection procedures, training, management development schemes, indeed a company's whole personnel policy contributes to the setting of standards and the prevention of disciplinary problems. The most successful disciplinary policy is one which provides excellent procedures but minimises the occasions for their use.

5 Procedures on other matters

137 The procedures for settling terms and conditions of employment, for dealing with grievances, for maintaining discipline are all of important concern to employees. But there are many other aspects of the day-to-day management of the workforce, closely affecting the interests of employees, where policy can be expressed and sustained through recognised procedures. A whole range of manpower policies from recruitment to retirement are of this kind.

138 The first requirement is to have a policy to express; a policy, for example, on the engagement of employees with related recruitment and selection procedures; on employee development with related induction, training, transfer and promotion procedures; a policy on terminations expressed through retirement and redundancy procedures. The formulation and adoption of policies on these matters is a management responsibility; the procedures to give effect to them are also commonly regarded as equally a management responsibility to be laid down and operated solely by management. But increasingly with the growth of employee organisation and the acknowledgement of employee interest in the operation of manpower policies there has been a development of jointly agreed procedures in these areas. This chapter reports on a number of such developments observed during the inquiries.

139 The basic purpose of unions to protect the interests of their members and to protect the union's continuing capacity to represent those interests accounts for many features of recruitment procedures which have been shaped by union pressures. From the early days of craft unions restriction of recruitment to union members has been a union policy objective in order to protect craft standards, negotiated terms and conditions and union power. The closed shop in its varying forms is an outcome of these actions. In its pre-entry form, as for example in some sections of the printing industry, the union becomes the source of labour supply and largely takes over the recruitment function. Management renunciation of the recruitment function into the hands of employees need not necessarily be the result of strong union organisation or the closed shop. This has happened in recent years where firms employing immigrant labour have found it convenient partly because of language problems, to look to the spokesmen of their existing employees to supply additional labour and have effectively, though not always with complete awareness, lost control of recruitment.

140 Closed shop arrangements vary considerably in the degree and form of union influence on the recruitment procedure. In some of the cases observed the union nominated candidates for vacancies and the field of candidates was restricted to that source; in some such cases only a single candidate was nominated leaving the employer with a formal option to appoint that person or leave the vacancy unfilled. In other cases the employer was free to find candidates in whatever way he wished, for example by advertisement in the press or through the offices of the Employment Service Agency. During the interviews candidates would be informed that if engaged they would be required to join the union — whether before or after appointment was often of secondary importance. In some cases candidates were introduced to a union representative after their interview with management, in others a new employee did not meet the union representative until after appointment.

141 In the main, closed shop arrangements were unwritten, but the following are two examples of written agreements. In one (in printing and publishing) labour was to be provided by the union subject to the condition that if the union failed to supply a candidate within a given time limit after a vacancy occurred management could fill the vacancy provided the person appointed became a member of the union. In the other, in the ports industry, it was laid down that half the candidates for a post would be nominated by the unions, the other half by management, and there was provision for a joint selection panel. Other examples elsewhere of joint management-union selection panels were encountered.

142 A highly-developed example of jointly agreed arrangements for recruitment and labour supply is provided by the Merchant Navy Established Service Scheme. This was established and is jointly supervised by the British Shipping Federation and the seafarers' unions for regulating entry of workers into the shipping industry by a system of registration and an employment service administered through regional and local offices. The British Shipping Federation provide staff for the administration of the scheme and the National Union of Seamen has representation on the network of joint district maritime boards which supervise registration and engagement and recruitment of seamen.

143 A jointly agreed arrangement to ease the manpower problems of the electrical contracting industry which suffers from seasonal unemployment is the establishment by the Joint Industry Board of an 'employment pool'. This is a voluntary arrangement. A worker who is available for employment informs the JIB which places him on the 'pool' list which is accessible to employers who are looking for labour.

144 Union interest in apprenticeship schemes affects pay negotiations and training procedures but it also has an important influence on recruitment procedures expressed through agreements on eligibility for selection and on ratios of apprentices to adult workers.

145 The procedural aspects of recruitment extend to complex arrangements to meet manpower planning requirements and cover a wide range of selection techniques but attention has been concentrated here on union influence on recruitment procedures as this is the aspect of particular concern for industrial relations. By some that influence may be regarded as purely restrictive and self-interested but that is by no means the view taken by all employers. Some are able to find common ground with unions on such matters as appropriate qualifications, preference for former employees, selection methods, apprentice ratios or a closed shop policy and consider that they benefit by bringing matters on which agreement can be found within the ambit of jointly agreed procedures. Such a favourable view was, not surprisingly, found only within the context of generally harmonious industrial relations.

146 Union interest in recruitment procedures is partly prompted by their concern with job security. That concern is directly involved when there is a threat of redundancy. In reporting on the inquiry findings on redundancy procedures a distinction is made between contingency arrangements and *ad hoc* arrangements. Contingency arrangements are defined as those made in anticipation of future reductions in manpower. Since they relate to a future and not an actual or imminent problem, they are necessarily concerned more with the principles of conduct than with details. *Ad hoc* arrangements are defined as those tailored to meet a specific problem, arising for example from a proposal to introduce new machinery, or from an adverse trading development. Such *ad hoc* arrangements, however, often set a precedent for future redundancies.

147 Inquiries were made to establish at whose instigation redundancy agreements or procedures were introduced.

148 In the case of contingency arrangements, there were a number of organisations in which management had devised redundancy policies and procedures which were incorporated in personnel handbooks or in guideline documents issued to managers. In some cases these policies and procedures had the tacit support of the unions though they had declined to be a party to them. In one company in printing and publishing the unions had been invited to join in discussions on redundancy provisions but refused. If at any time management had any proposals to make that might affect manpower the unions would listen to them, but they would react strictly in the light of those proposals and prevailing circumstances. They preferred to reserve their position completely. In another company in cable-making there was the reverse situation. The management had set out general principles for the handling of redundancy and the unions were pressing for a much more specific joint agreement. Management had however refused this on the grounds that a more specific agreement would make it difficult to take into account the circumstances of a particular redundancy.

149 There were however companies in which contingency arrangements had been incorporated into jointly-agreed procedures, sometimes on the union's initiative, sometimes the management's. In one company contingency arrangements for redundancy were one element in a jointly determined major reconstruction of industrial relations. The redundancy agreement set out the principles for dealing with the effects upon manpower of a decline in production and required the parties to meet to formulate specific plans when the circumstances made it necessary. Both the management and the shop stewards in that company reported that the redundancy agreement had enabled them to weather a number of major trade crises to their mutual and separate satisfaction.

150 In the case of *ad hoc* redundancy arrangements, it was usually management who, faced with a recession in trade or wishing to introduce technological or organisational change, made proposals to the unions concerning redundancy implications. In one case in printing and publishing the management informed the union that the introduction of new machines was imminent and suggested a meeting to negotiate a redundancy agreement. The union refused to have any discussions at all unless there was a prior guarantee of no redundancy. In most other *ad hoc* cases, however, the unions were prepared to enter into discussions and to agree upon principles (eg 'last in, first out') and methods for dealing with displaced employees.

151 There is ample scope for joint discussion of measures which might be taken to mitigate the effects of a reduction in manpower. The following examples are some of those noted:

(a) Cessation of recruitment

(b) Cessation of contracting work out

(c) Short-time working

(d) Work-sharing

(e) Consultation with other employers in the area

(f) Early warning to and consultation with the local offices of the Employment Service Agency

(g) Redeployment within the organisation

(h) Re-training for transferred employees

(i) Voluntary early retirement for those over a certain age

(j) Voluntary redundancy.

Not all these measures are likely to be suitable in all circumstances. For example, there may be no work contracted out in the first place. If the anticipated reduction in manpower is deemed to be permanent, short-time working and work-sharing may not be appropriate. What matters is that all posible measures should be systematically considered and joint discussion often generates new ideas.

152 Such measures were found in schemes operated solely by management and in joint procedures. In the case of joint procedures, in both contingency arrangements and in a procedure designed to meet a specific situation, the chronological order in which the measures were to be taken had often been a matter for negotiation. Steps to redeploy and re-train displaced employees featured high in the unions' priorities. In one agreement a distinction was drawn between a reduction in manpower due to reasons within the company's control and a reduction for reasons outside it. The procedure in the two cases was different.

153 A number of unions who were party to joint procedures reported that agreement upon the means of dealing with manpower reductions had the effect of considerably reducing and in some cases eliminating altogether the need for any compulsory redundancies. This was usually achieved by exploiting to the full all the possibilities for redeployment, voluntary early retirement and voluntary redundancy.

154 Agreements on redundancies often have both procedural and substantive aspects. The substantive element can include compensation payments to redundant employees and re-settlement and temporary travel allowances for transferred (i e redeployed) employees. In some public sector industries compensation and other monetary terms were negotiated at industry level. The amount paid in compensation (over and above the requirements of the Redundancy Payments Act) can have a significant effect on the smooth handling of a redundancy operation. The level of payment may, for example, encourage voluntary redundancy and increase the acceptability of temporary transfers. The money element and the procedural steps in these as in other types of agreement are often inter-related parts of a single agreement.

155 In some cases there was a special appeals procedure to deal with employee grievances arising out of a redeployment or redundancy operation; in other cases such appeals were dealt with through the normal grievance/disputes procedure.

156 A general manpower policy which aims to make effective use of employees and promote their contentment with the way their interests are considered in the running of the organisation may include a whole range of policies on such subjects as induction, transfers, training, productivity and promotion, all with their related procedures. Like other procedures they may be laid down by the management or they may be the outcome of joint discussions undertaken to elicit employee opinion and ideas and to secure employee co-operation.

157 Promotion is a subject on which employees can be expected to have strong opinions. Where these are reflected in jointly agreed procedures they commonly take the form of jointly agreed provisions to secure fair consideration of the claims of eligible candidates leaving the actual selection to be made by the management. Where there is an agreed rule that promotion shall be made by seniority the choice is governed by the procedure but such arrangements are normally confined to relatively junior jobs where a selection procedure would not be likely to produce very different results.

158 Jointly agreed promotion procedures have long been a feature of staffing policy in the public service and are normal throughout the public sector. Where they were found in the private sector they usually formed some part of a jointly agreed job-grading or job-evaluation scheme often involving joint consideration of cases. Promotion procedures cover such items as general notification of vacant posts, the definition of eligible candidates, methods of applying for consideration, reports on candidates, sifting of applications, interview arrangements, promulgation of results and appeals.

159 Although management normally make the selection from eligible candidates unions influence the selection process when the procedure provides for determining eligibility. One common restriction is a provision giving prior, preferential consideration to candidates within the organisation. Another is to limit the field of eligible candidates by imposing seniority or length of service conditions. In one organisation there was joint agreement upon the job specification for vacant posts as they occurred. In a number of organisations there was an agreement that both sides would submit an equal number of nominations for promotion to a vacant post, though in practice this often amounted simply to agreeing the short-list of candidates.

160 One large public sector undertaking did make provision for union representatives to sit with management on a selection panel. This was in an industry-level agreement. At operating levels in the organisation, however, it was rare for unions to exercise this right. They preferred to influence the final choice in a number of ways which fell short of sharing in the final choice, for example by agreeing the job description or agreeing on who should be candidates for the post. This left the union free to take up the case of employees who wished to appeal against not having been promoted.

161 The most common form of appeals procedure was for appeals against not being promoted. In one local authority this took the form of a joint management-union investigating committee. In addition there were procedures for appealing against non-inclusion in a short-list of candidates. This entailed publishing the list of candidates in sufficient time for appeals to be registered and heard before interviewing took place. In one location in the industrial Civil Service a permanent 'potential promotion list' was maintained, for promotion from shop floor to supervisor, and there was an appeals procedure against non-inclusion in this list. When vacancies occurred there was thus no delay through hearing appeals before action to fill the vacancies was taken.

162 The best man for the job is a commonly expressed management objective in promotions policy. Unions tend to emphasise the claims of seniority. These views are not irreconcilable. In assessing suitability management will wish to give some weight to experience and will also wish to consider the effect of appointments on successful team working. Unions, while usually content to leave the promotion decisions to management, will wish to secure consideration for senior employees who have built up promotion expectations and also a procedure which is demonstrably not purely arbitrary. Considerations of this sort have shaped promotion procedures which give some allowance for seniority both in defining the field of eligible candidates and in assessing the claims of contenders for promotion. Seniority limitations in such procedures tend to diminish or disappear with higher grades.

163 The most senior appointments are outside the ambit of negotiated procedures though in the public sector agreed procedures apply to grades for which in the private sector they would normally be regarded as quite unsuitable. A procedure may well apply to promotion to a grade immediately above those grades for which representational rights are acknowledged on the argument that what the procedure deals with is not the appointment to be made but proper consideration of the claims of those in the grade from which the appointment is made.

164 Training is important for the efficient running of an organisation and for career development, and management and employees both have an interest in the amount and type of training provided and the way in which it is organised. There were many examples of joint discussion of training programmes. In some types of training such as induction training and industrial relations training union representatives participated both as instructors and as students. In relation to technical training the union's interest was similar to its interest in promotion in seeking an agreed procedure providing equitable access to training opportunities. This was of particular importance in one company employing a sizeable proportion of Asian workers where a jointly-agreed procedure for selection for training was one of the measures introduced to meet allegations of discrimination.

165 The sentiments of employees about equitable access to promotion and training opportunities are matched by their feelings about equitable arrangements to meet the less agreeable requirements of manpower deployment. In one large organisation with a number of scattered offices temporary transfers away from home were needed from time to time to meet local staffing shortages. The selection was made in accordance with a jointly-agreed procedure setting out the categories governing the order of transfer from volunteers to those with the heaviest local commitments. Cases of particular hardship were the subject of a special appeals procedure. In another large undertaking there was a temporary transfer procedure which stipulated where and how a transferred employee should be placed on the grading scales and the circumstances which would allow temporary upgrading.

166 Other examples of special procedures negotiated to meet manning problems were the 'changeover procedure' in the paper making industry to deal with changes from three-shift to four-shift working and a 'call-in' procedure negotiated in a company in that industry setting out the arrangements for calling in men from home to make up numbers on machines whose operation required a certain manning level. Complaints arising from the operation of this procedure were dealt with separately from the general grievance procedure. In the public transport industry agreed procedures required a fixed period of advance notice to the union before changes in running schedules became effective thus providing time for consultation which in practice often resulted in negotiated changes.

167 The procedures mentioned in this chapter illustrate the point that the range and scope of jointly agreed procedures follows the range and scope of subject matter brought within the ambit of joint discussion. With the elaboration of specialised procedural arrangements, often with their own appeals procedure, the load of business falling on a general grievance procedure is reduced and can often be more effectively dispatched.

6 The role of third parties in procedures

168 It is for employers and employees to settle how they will conduct their mutual relations. Nobody can do this for them but this does not mean that how they do the job is of no concern to others nor that the parties themselves do not from time to time look for and welcome assistance. This chapter examines some of the forms which third party involvement takes.

169 'Third party' is a term which employers who do not recognise trade unions often apply to unions in the frequent comment: 'I don't want a third party coming between me and my employees'. For our purposes the principal parties are the employer and his employees including representatives acting on behalf of either; a third party seeks to assist both the principal parties and is normally required to be free of commitment to the interests of either. However, in cases moving from the domestic to the external stages of an agreed procedure the representatives of the principal parties may also be representing the wider interests of other related employers and employees. They need to combine support for the interests of the principal parties who are their members with that degree of detachment from partisan involvement in the particular issue dividing them which is the characteristic contribution which third parties can make to the resolution of disputes.

170 Assistance in the resolution of disputes is the commonest activity of third parties and the various forms of this activity are the main subject matter of this chapter. Dispute resolution is not however by any means the only way in which third party action influences procedures. Employers, trade unions and the State have all been active in providing not only conciliation and arbitration services to assist in the resolution of disputes but advisory services to assist in the development of better procedures.

171 The most powerful third party is the State. Procedures to improve standards of health and safety at work were imposed by State action and have subsequently been greatly developed by voluntary joint action of employers and unions with the active encouragement of the State's inspectors. Where organisation has been weak and pay low, the State has intervened to set up Wages Councils with procedures for the determination and enforcement of minimum rates of pay and holiday entitlements. In the docks comprehensive procedures for the registration, deployment, and discipline of dock labour have been established by statute. For the most part however, the State's influence on industrial relations procedures has been exercised through its powers of inquiry, political advocacy, economic inducement, example and the provision of services. The system of collective bargaining with joint regulation of procedural matters has been commended by the Whitley and Donovan reports, advocated and practised by governments, prescribed by statute as a policy obligation to nationalised industries and encouraged through the embodiment in government contracts of the Fair Wages Resolution of the House of Commons. To assist the operation of the system the State has made available to the principal parties a wide range of conciliation, arbitration and advisory services.

172 Advice on instituting, developing and improving procedures for the conduct of industrial relations has for many years been provided by the Department of Employment both in publications and by its industrial relations staff. This function, together with the staff, has now been transferred to the Advisory, Conciliation and Arbitration Service. Procedural reform was the essence of the work of the Commission on Industrial Relations and is a principal feature in most of its ninety published reports. Advice does not flow only from official sources. Employers organisations, trade unions, professional bodies, academics, consultants advise their members, clients or readers on the operation and improvement of procedures. It is a subject which features frequently in conference programmes and is a staple item in the curriculum of industrial relations training courses.

173 Advisory services are in general intended to be of long-term effect and may be remote from immediate issues, although advice in particular cases, like many of the CIR investigations in individual companies, may relate to situations of some urgency. Conciliation and arbitration are always concerned with immediate issues. The role of the conciliator is to assist parties in dispute to reach agreement. He provides a channel of communication when direct communication has broken down or become ineffective, he canvasses possible new approaches, he defines common ground and remaining points of difference, he provides the parties with assessments of the situation, he does everything in his power to promote agreement but he is the midwife and not the parent of any agreement eventually reached. The mediator performs a similar service but in addition will be prepared if necessary to propose his own solution in a final bid to provide a basis for the ultimately necessary agreement. The distinction is a fine one and often blurred in practice. A mediator proceeds by way of conciliation and may not need to do more; a conciliator, although not officially identified with a particular solution, will nevertheless know how to let his own views influence the parties. The arbitrator's job is to make an award determining an issue after considering the submissions of the parties.

174 Conciliation and arbitration facilities have been provided by the State at public expense since the Conciliation Act 1896 and extended in subsequent legislation. The Department of Employment carried out most of the conciliation work directly through its own specialist staff as a day-to-day public service although outside conciliators were appointed from time to time for particular cases. Arbitration was never undertaken by departmental staff. Cases were remitted to the Industrial Court established by statute in 1919 or other specialist tribunals, arbitration boards or single arbitrators. The Department's role was to see that the arbitral bodies were maintained and serviced. The award was to the parties and not to the Department. Recently the conciliation and arbitration functions have been transferred to the Advisory, Conciliation and Arbitration Service. In addition to the officially provided services there are a number of arrangements for third party help established independently by joint agreement in particular industries.

175 The involvement of a third party does not mean that the issue passes out of the hands of the principal parties. Conciliators and mediators help but do not decide. Arbitrators decide but only within the limits and subject to the conditions agreed by the parties, apart from cases brought under Section 8 of the Terms and Conditions of Employment Act, 1959, cases involving interpretation of the Fair Wages Resolution and the statutory provisions for arbitration for teachers and the police. Generally there is prior agreement by the parties to accept an arbitrator's award and even when this is not explicit there is normally a recognised obligation to accept the award as determining the issue; in some cases however the agreement extends only to seeking the arbitrator's verdict, the final resolution of the issue depending on subsequent agreement between the parties. Strictly, such a process cannot be regarded as arbitration but rather as an inquiry with recommendations. Even where, as in the Civil Service, there are standing arrangements for arbitration at the instance of either party with prior agreement to accept the outcome, the whole process is dependent on the continued maintenance of the joint agreement which brought it into being. Apart from the special cases mentioned arbitration in this country is not an alternative to joint agreement. It is the jointly agreed method which the parties choose for settling issues which they define in accordance with conditions which both accept.

176 The assistance which third parties can give to the principal parties is recognised and provided for in many joint agreements. These take many forms. Industry- or service-wide procedures normally provide for a joint panel to render assistance by way of conciliation or arbitration to lower levels involved in a dispute. 96 per cent of the agreements examined had some such provision. In practice the conciliation and arbitration processes are often not clearly distinguished and the joint panels may continue to negotiate the dispute. Much depends on their prescribed authority and the practice which has developed. In the rubber industry, for example, a conciliation panel consisting of two management and two union representatives involved in the dispute, is confined by the joint agreement to dealing with matters not related to the interpretation of the national agreement. Similarly constituted disputes committees in the chemical industry make binding awards.

177 Nine per cent of the industry level agreements examined had provision for an independent chairman of the industry level conciliation panel. He has a particular responsibility to help resolve issues should the other members of the panel be divided. In the knitting and in the commercial printing industries the chairman has a conciliation role. In textiles the chairman is empowered to make binding recommendations should his efforts to conciliate fail.

178 In the docks there are examples of specialised local arbitration undertaken by joint teams from areas not involved in the issue. These arose out of the supersession of piecework by payments systems related less closely to output, introduced as a result of the second Devlin Report. In the London Enclosed Docks arbitration takes place on disputes over the time required to shift a particular cargo. In Bristol payments for 'abnormal cargoes and conditions' are subject to on the spot arbitration if they cannot be agreed. These provisions are similar in character to those provided for the investigation of manning problems in the coal industry.

179 Another specialised third party provision is found in the shipbuilding industry. The national demarcation agreement provides for local panels of six outside arbitrators to be set up by the Secretary of State for Employment in consultation with the parties; when agreement cannot be reached on a demarcation dispute it is referred automatically by management to the regional representative of the Department of Employment (now transferred to the ACAS) who selects an arbitrator from the panel.

180 The Joint Industry Board of the electrical contracting industry has its own officers who are independent of either side. The local joint board, can arbitrate at local level on non-national matters but in practice many disputes are solved through conciliation undertaken by the board's officers outside written procedures.

181 Official arrangements in the public sector tend to be formal though practices differ widely. In the British Steel Corporation the first stage of the disputes procedure beyond works level is the Neutral Committee.

This consists of two representatives of the unions and two of management who are unaffected by the dispute and a representative of the Corporation. The Committee produces a 'memorandum of settlement' which is usually accepted.

182 In the electricity supply industry and in the National Health Service regional appeals committees, consisting of joint management/union panels made up of people from other areas from that in which the dispute occurred, are used as a form of arbitration though their decisions can be appealed against. In electricity supply this procedure is used for disciplinary matters only and is subject to a final appeal to an arbitrator appointed by the Department of Employment assisted by two assessors appointed by the parties. In the National Health Service the regional appeals committee deals only with individual grievances, usually grading appeals.

183 In a number of the examples quoted arbitration arrangements have been agreed to deal with a particular type of issue. There is much to commend this approach. Parties are often unwilling to commit themselves to remit to third party judgement broad issues affecting their vital interests but the same considerations need not apply to more limited issues such as disciplinary cases. Thought can usefully be directed to identifying issues which might be more suitable than others for resolution by arbitration. The national demarcation agreement in the shipbuilding industry is a good example of this approach.

184 It is sometimes suggested that an appropriate field for greater use of arbitration could be established by distinguishing differences of right from differences of interest on lines familiar in the United States. On this approach terms and conditions of employment would be settled in negotiations by the parties but any disputes regarding the interpretation of agreements between the parties would be determined by arbitration. In general this is not a distinction which is clearly present in the minds and practice of negotiators in this country as reflected in the agreements they make. Substantive consequences of some importance may turn on questions of interpretation and the intentions of the parties on any disputed matter are seen by the parties as a further question of interest for discussion and settlement by them rather than as matters of construction of the terms of the written agreement. To use the distinction between questions of right and questions of interest as a general basis for defining arbitrable issues would require fundamental changes in the nature and status of collective agreements. It is however a distinction which may be useful to parties who are seeking to identify and define arbitrable issues within their own agreements.

185 The appeal of arbitration as a reasonable means for rational determination of all disputes is often felt more strongly by those who suffer indirectly from the consequences of industrial strife than by the parties directly involved. One or other or both parties may readily accept the use of arbitration on particular occasions or for a particular type of issue but parties are in general unwilling to accept a general commitment to use arbitration as a final stage in negotiating procedure. It is argued not only that such a commitment involves an unacceptable renunciation of responsibility but that it weakens the incentive to reach an agreed settlement and distorts the negotiating process by directing the attention and tactics of the parties to a possible arbitration hearing rather than to a possible agreement.

186 Some agreements provide for 'independents' to be used at a certain stage in the procedure. The most elaborate of these is the 'conciliation' scheme of the coalmining industry which provides three levels of binding arbitration to correspond with three different levels of settlement for different types of issue. At pit level there is an umpire, at area level a referee and nationally a three-man national reference tribunal appointed by the Master of the Rolls. These appointments are permanent. The system differs markedly from the provisions of the 1966 Power Loading Agreement for investigation of manning disputes by a four-man joint team drawn from the same district.

187 Specialised arbitration tribunals are provided for by agreement in the Post Office, non-industrial Civil Service, London Transport and British Rail and by legislation for teachers and the police. In the National Health Service, local authorities and the industrial Civil Service cases are dealt with by the official arbitration agencies provided for general use. All the permanent tribunals provide for independent chairmen but provision for the 'side' members varies. The Police Act 1969 provides for 'three arbitrators appointed by the Prime Minister'. The Civil Service Arbitration Tribunal and the Post Office Arbitration Tribunal consist of a chairman appointed by the Secretary of State for Employment; the chairman chooses a side member from each of the two representative panels drawn up by the Secretary of State after consultation with the parties. Teaching, British Rail and London Transport all have arbitration bodies with chairmen appointed by the Secretary of State and side members nominated by the parties.

188 Appointments of members of arbitral bodies in the public sector have in the past normally been made by the Secretary of State for Employment but the Master of the Rolls appoints the members of the National Reference Tribunal of the coalmining industry. In the private sector it is normal for the parties to make the appointments, often of individuals about whom they are agreed or on the basis of suggestions put forward by the ACAS. In the clearing banks by agreement the President of the Law Society makes the appointments.

189 A common characteristic of those acting as conciliators or arbitrators, or as chairmen of conciliation or arbitration bodies, is dissociation from employer or union interests. 'Independent' or 'neutral' are the adjectives usually applied to the role and the practitioners are for the most part lawyers, academics or civil servants whose work or special interests and personality make them suitable for the job and acceptable to the parties. But neutrality in this sense is not invariably a requirement for third parties and a number of managers and trade unionists have established a personal reputation of neutrality on issues in which they cannot be regarded as having a direct interest. The local conferences of the engineering industry disputes procedure used to provide for manual workers and still provide for non-manual workers a form of what has been called 'employer conciliation' by drawing in employers from other areas. The Engineering Employers' Federation (EEF) has claimed the same virtues for it as for the use of a joint body of 'independents'.

> 'The essence of (Local conference) is that it brings new minds and wider experience to bear on the issue raised . . . The rate of settlement at this stage of procedure is high'.
> (Written evidence of EEF to Donovan Commission, paras 169–170).

The system is also found in the paper and board industry. A somewhat similar appeal to the committed but uninvolved occurs when a works committee on which all unions are represented is involved as a stage in procedure in a case brought by one of them.

190 The examples quoted illustrate the very wide variety of forms which third party involvement in procedures takes. Often the variations, like the variations in procedures generally, merely reflect the chances of historical development. Sometimes the particular form adopted is governed by the concern of the parties to ensure that their affairs are dealt with by someone whom they can trust to know their circumstances. Distance from involvement in the disputed issue is highly desirable but remoteness from the technicalities, circumstances and practices of the industry can prove a handicap. The appointment of assessors is one way of avoiding this danger. Another is the use of specialised tribunals where the volume of business makes this practicable.

191 The need for variety of forms, for expert knowledge, for adaptations to meet the wishes of parties is well recognised in the public provision made for third party assistance. The Industrial Courts Act 1919 not only established the Industrial Court as a permanent, independent tribunal to assist parties seeking adjudication of a disputed issue but also provided for arbitration by single arbitrators or by boards of arbitration consisting of persons nominated by the parties under an independent chairman nominated by the Minister. It was under the powers contained in this Act that a specialised body in the form of the Post Office Arbitration Tribunal was constituted to meet the agreed wishes of the parties. The conciliation service by the very nature of its operations is highly flexible in its methods and fertile in suggesting a limitless range of procedural devices suited to the circumstances of particular cases.

192 It is easy to overestimate the importance of third party involvement as a procedural step. It can of course be very important in the resolution of particular cases but the volume of business involving third parties is minute compared with the volume of business transacted solely by the principal parties. The fact that extensive provision is made for recourse to third parties both in legislation and in industry-wide agreements should not mask the relative rarity of the use of those provisions. Important cases involving third party intervention attract wide publicity; the institutional arrangements lend themselves to study and exposition which may magnify their actual role. But overwhelmingly the normal experience of the operation of procedures is confined to the principal parties. The relative rarity of the use of official arbitration is illustrated by the following figures.

193 The number of cases heard by five of the specialised arbitral bodies in the public sector in the years 1963–74 was as shown in table 1.

Table 1

Year	Civil Service Arb. Trib.	Post Office Arb. Trib. (established 1970)	Teachers' arbit'n.	Elec Supply appeals Tri. (established 1969)	Rly. Staffs Nat. Trib.
1963	19		0		0
1964	8		0		8
1965	8		1		4
1966	6		0		1
1967	6		1		0
1968	12		2		0
1969	4		2	0	1
1970	1	0	1	7	0
1971	6	3	2	4	0
1972	3	7	2	12	0
1973	0	3	0	5	0
1974	1	0	0	5	2

194 Statistics for the Industrial Court (since 1971 the Industrial Arbitration Board), for Boards of Arbitration and for single arbitrators over the same period are as shown in table 2.

Table 2

Year	Industrial Court	Boards	Single	Totals
1963	36	1	32	69
1964	35	0	24	59
1965	19	9	39	67
1966	22	2	43	67
1967	7	0	27	34
1968	12	2	42	56
1969	14	4	41	59
1970	9	4	48	61
1971	7	8	48	63
1972	15	17	48	80
1973	5	4	50	59
1974	8	17	127	152
Totals	189	68	569	826

195 The extent of the activities of the conciliation service is difficult to measure statistically as much informal conciliation work is undertaken as part of the general advisory service. The official records refer only to formal conciliation. Over the period 1964 to 1974 the numbers of disputes subject to formal conciliation were as follows:

1964	1965	1966	1967	1968	1969	1970	1971	1972	1973	1974
408	406	447	413	412	516	647	650	716	866	1235

196 Well over half the cases going to arbitration concerned pay. For the conciliation service recognition disputes and pay disputes each accounted for some 37 per cent of cases and 13 per cent were over redundancy and dismissals.

197 98 per cent of the industry-level agreements analysed provided for third party assistance to the principal parties which in 21 per cent was automatic on failure to agree at the previous stage but the general view among employers associations was that relatively little use was made of these provisions. The emphasis was on domestic settlement and assistance from the association was often directed to achieving domestic settlements. Comprehensive statistics were not available.

198 Normally settlements require the agreement of both principal parties. The wartime Industrial Disputes Order providing for an enforceable settlement at the instance of one only of the principal parties was discontinued in 1959. The intervention of the National Board for Prices and Incomes under the Prices and Incomes Acts 1966 to 1968 was not directed to making a settlement but to pronouncing on whether actual or prospective settlements between principal parties were in conformity with prescribed criteria as a basis for possible government action to forbid the operation of the settlement. The provisions in the Industrial Relations Act 1971 for prescribing an enforceable procedure were never operated. Some of the possible reasons for this are discussed in the final chapter.

199 There is an abundance of provisions for third party assistance to principal parties both by way of officially provided services and through the terms of national agreements. They take a wide variety of forms and are flexible and adaptable to circumstances. They often prove to be a valuable instrument for dealing with major troubles and for oiling the machinery of collective bargaining. But their role is ancillary and in quantitative terms, minor. Procedures are essentially about relations between employers and their employees. It is inevitably in that domestic context that they mainly exist and that the decisions are taken which determine whether they shall flourish or fail. It was with this conviction in mind that the Donovan Commission put primary emphasis on the improvement of domestic procedures and made one of its principal recommendations the creation of a new-style third party agency, the Commission on Industrial Relations, which would be concerned not with the prompt settlement of particular disputes but with long-term structural reform and the provision of a central agency for the dissemination of information and advice on procedural reform. It is a function which now comes within the ambit of the ACAS alongside its responsibilities for conciliation and arbitration.

7 Commitment to use procedure

200 Where jointly agreed procedures have been introduced questions arise about which matters are subject to the procedure and about restrictions on unilateral action by managements and unions pending completion of action under the procedure. They are related questions. A complaint that unilateral action is a breach of procedure may be met by a contention that the procedure does not apply to the case.

201 Restraints on independent action by one or both of the parties to a procedure agreement often take the form of a clause prohibiting hostile action whilst an issue is 'in procedure'. The industry procedure agreements analysed showed the following percentage distribution of such clauses:

Clause prohibiting strike action (in some cases industrial action short of a strike also)	24
No lock-out clause	0
Both a no-strike and a no-lockout clause	41
Neither	35
	100

Thus 65 per cent industry-wide procedures contain a clause of some kind prohibiting hostile action more commonly taking the form of both a no-strike and a no-lock-out clause. An examination of the less comprehensive information on domestic agreements showed a similar pattern.

202 A dispute may remain unresolved for weeks, giving the parties plenty of time to consider, from their respective standpoints, the implications of recourse to industrial action or, if there are any, to procedures beyond domestic level. But an issue may erupt into industrial action with great rapidity. Senior management's first intimation of trouble may in fact be a report that industrial action is already being taken. How effective are no-strike clauses in preventing industrial action before procedure is exhausted?

203 If a group of workers with a powerful sense of grievance has decided to strike, neither management nor their own union officials or representatives are likely to deter them from striking by invoking a no-strike clause. Nevertheless, both managements and unions attached importance to no-strike clauses, even in the more strike-prone industries investigated. The main value of a no-strike clause was seen as a symbol of commitment to resolving issues by negotiation. It indicates the method by which the grievance will have to be dealt with and concentrates efforts on the restoration of that method. But if repair and restoration jobs become frequent it is an indication that the system of industrial relations in operation is in need of fundamental review. In some circumstances a no-strike clause may merely symbolise an ineffective attempt to tackle symptoms rather than causes.

204　Another form of establishing a commitment to the use of procedure is found in *status quo* clauses. In broad terms such a clause in a procedure agreement seeks to establish that changes in working conditions which affect employee interests will not, if challenged, be put into effect until agreement has been reached between the parties or the full agreed procedure for the resolution of disputes has been exhausted. The problems in seeking to negotiate such a clause have mainly arisen over the extent and manner of its application particularly in relation to questions of labour utilisation. In national level negotiations for manual workers in the engineering industry difficulties in defining what precisely such a clause was intended to cover and how it was to be invoked led to the suspension of the negotiations and the abrogation of the national procedure agreement for the avoidance of disputes.

205　The CBI[1] and the TUC have both commented on *status quo* provisions but with different indications of how the principle is to be applied. The CBI, after noting that some matters were accepted as clearly appropriate for management decision and others as clearly appropriate for negotiation, added 'But there will be a grey area in between, whose nature may change in course of time as both methods and attitudes change, where the unions may disagree with management's view that it has the right to make unilateral decisions'. Whether or not it was possible or desirable to treat such developments by specific agreement was not a matter on which it was possible to generalise. Industries and companies would be wise to consider whether the inclusion of *status quo* provisions in their procedure agreements would contribute to an improvement in industrial relations. 'Where it is decided that the inclusion of *status quo* provisions would be likely to be beneficial, it is important that both the matters to be susceptible to the provisions, and the nature of the *status quo* to be observed should be defined as precisely as possible'. In general introductory comment on the subject the CBI observed that where joint

---

[1] 'Disputes Procedures' CBI 1970, pp 22-27

consultation 'is practised with goodwill the demarcation between consultation of a purely advisory character and negotiation, where workpeople's representatives play a part in decision making, becomes insignificant and the need for formal *status quo* provisions disappears . . . The more effective consultation is in practice, the more the suspicions that give rise to demands for the *status quo* will be allayed'.

206 The TUC consider that the maintenance of the *status quo* would be conductive to industrial peace[1], and cite the speed-up of work, dismissals, manning arrangements and redundancy as examples where a *status quo* provision is necessary. In the interim report by the TUC General Council on industrial democracy for the 1973 Trades Union Congress[2] the following recommendation was made on procedures:

> 'A major extension of collective bargaining to matters involving work organisation would need to be accompanied by the widespread adoption of procedural arrangements which incorporate some form of mutual *status quo* arrangements. This restricts the ability of management to introduce changes outside negotiated or customary practice'.

207 The CBI considers that the areas to be subject to a *status quo* clause and the nature of the *status quo* ought to be 'defined as precisely as possible'; the TUC sees the *status quo* principle as restricting the ability of management to introduce changes 'outside negotiated or customary practice'.

208 *Status quo* clauses take several forms. They may be directly related to a no-strike clause, the union giving an undertaking not to withdraw labour or engage in industrial action until the machinery for settling disputes has been exhausted and the employer accepting that the '*status quo* during this time will prevail'. Sometimes, however, particularly in procedures specialising in one type of issue such as discipline, the particular matters subject to a *status quo* provision are listed.

209 One method of defining the application of a *status quo* provision in a procedure agreement is to relate it to any matter in respect of which the procedure is invoked. Thus a proposed 'complaints' procedure for a particular dockyard's industrial grades simply stated that

> 'The conditions existing prior to those which brought about the complaint will apply throughout the procedure'.

---

[1] 'Programme for action', TUC 1969 p8.
[2] 'Supplementary Report B', para 68.

Similarly the application of a *status quo* clause in a substantive agreement may be related to the terms and conditions covered by the agreement. An example is to be found in the Paper and Boardmaking national agreement for process and general workers:

> 'No alteration shall be made in the wages and conditions of any class of workers other than as provided in this agreement except after consideration of an application submitted to the District Board of the Federation and the union'.

210   In some clauses it is not only those matters subject to a written agreement which are covered by the *status quo* clause but also those where an 'established practice' exists which are brought within its scope. The clause proposed by the Confederation of Shipbuilding and Engineering Unions (CSEU) at national level for the engineering industry went further by seeking to make all alterations in established wages, working conditions and manning levels subject to joint agreement or the exhaustion of procedure.

211   A different approach to defining scope of application is to specify the areas not subject to the *status quo* in the written agreement. An example was the 'management functions' clause in the 1922 procedure agreement for manual workers in the engineering industry:

> 'Questions arising which do not result in one class of workpeople being replaced by another in the establishment and on which discussion is desired shall be dealt with in accordance with the Provisions for Avoiding Disputes and work shall proceed meantime under the conditions following the act of management'.

212   In more than 200 national agreements in firms containing 300 or more employees in 27 industries only 17 per cent had *status quo* clauses. Most of these clauses were of a general nature, only 1 per cent referring to specific areas. Analysis of a selection of domestic procedure agreements showed 23 per cent with *status quo* clauses of which 6 per cent referred to specific matters the rest being of a general nature.

213   At domestic level, *status quo* agreements do not appear to vary much in frequency between public and private sector; company wide and plant level; and single and multi-union situations. In some industries, e g chemicals and engineering, *status quo* clauses are found oftener than in others, such as footwear and food, but this difference is only marginal. The greatest difference discernible is between agreements covering craft workers of which 35 per cent have *status quo* clauses compared with the more usual 20 per cent.

214 The *status quo* question has been a major issue in the engineering industry for many decades. It featured in the 1898 and 1922 settlements establishing procedures for the avoidance of disputes. It was the main issue leading to the abandonment of the disputes procedure for manual workers in 1972. It has provided a focus for contention over the general questions of managerial prerogatives and workers' rights and its history has reflected changes in the relative power positions of the parties.

215 The 1922 manual disputes procedure contained a limited but relatively well defined *status quo* provision. This established that no general alterations in wages, the working week or in working conditions that were subject to official agreement would be made by the employer until procedure had been exhausted. This provision was also included in later agreements with the white-collar unions. Much more significant was the inclusion in the 1922 procedure of the so-called 'managerial functions' clause quoted in para 211.

216 By the mid-sixties it was evident that the national procedure agreement needed revision. Constitutional strikes accounted for not much more than 5 per cent of all strikes by manual workers. Moreover there had been a gradual and continuous consolidation of union influence in a number of fields once considered to be exclusively matters for management decision. Despite the formal assertion of management prerogative in the 'management functions' clause of the national procedure agreement it was widely recognised in practice that where shop floor organisation was strong decisions concerning the organisation of the work and the arrangement of the labour force had to be negotiated.

217 A similar change in actual practice, reflecting changes in power relationships, was seen in the way the national agreement on piecework came to be operated. The agreement states that piecework job values 'shall be fixed by mutual arrangement between the employer and the worker who is to perform the job'. The agreement contains a provision stating that:

> 'Pending an arrangement being come to regarding a piecework price, bonus or basis time, the worker shall proceed with the job in accordance with the piecework price, bonus or basis time allowed by management'.

but this provision was not accepted by the AUEW, (Engineering Section), the National Society of Metal Mechanics and the Transport and General Workers' Union except in cases covered by established domestic arrangements. In post-war circumstances of full employment and strong shopfloor organisation the 'mutuality' provision in the national piecework agreement was developed by union officials and shop stewards as a major instrument for negotiating increased earnings while the practice of work proceeding meanwhile on the management's terms declined.

218 By the late 1960's the 'management functions' clause in the industry-wide procedure had ceased to have any practical meaning for large sectors of the engineering industry though the position differed markedly between different sectors and establishments according to the strength or weakness of trade union organisation. Discussions took place at industry level to try to reach agreement on a new national procedure agreement.

219 A new *status quo* formulation proposed by the EEF in June 1970 was:

'Where an employer takes a decision which is within the framework of an existing agreement or an established practice there shall be no obligation upon the employer to postpone the implementation of that decision until agreement has been reached or the procedure has been exhausted.

'On the other hand, where an employer takes a decision which means departure from a domestic agreement or an established practice, and the worker concerned objects to that decision, the employer shall be obliged to reach agreement or exhaust the procedure before implementing the decision'.

This formulation legitimised custom and practice and abandoned the 1922 'management functions' clause. The EEF considered that with the addition of a sentence to cover 'grey areas' where the interpretation might be open to some doubt the formulation came close to providing a basis for agreement.

220 By February 1971, however, it became clear that the union side were insisting on the original proposal submitted by the CSEU in October 1969. This stated that all alterations in established wages, working conditions and manning levels to which workers objected should be subject to mutuality or exhaustion of procedure. No agreement proved possible and in the event the old agreement was terminated without being replaced. Further discussions about a national procedure agreement have since taken place, but those of January 1973 were adjourned on the basis that either party could make an approach to the other if they had any further thoughts, particularly on the question of a *status quo* provision.

221 The EEF expressed its objections to open-ended clauses in the following extract from the Annual Review 1971/1972:

'The Federation has never denied the unions' right to question or seek to alter any management decision through the process of consultation and negotiation but it is not prepared to grant them the additional right to delay the implementation of any decision without discussion by the mere act of raising an objection'.

The EEF's proposed clause would limit the application of the *status quo* to decisions which imply 'departure from a domestic agreement or an established practice' the effect of the clause being conditioned by the practice in the establishment. The CSEU clause would apply to any change to established working conditions thus seeking to generalise for all establishments, and even to increase, the wide scope of collective bargaining achieved in those establishments where the unions were most powerful.

222 Those difficulties in achieving agreements on *status quo* provisions at national level which can be attributed to the wide variation of circumstances, policy and practice between different companies do not stand in the way of company agreements and a number of such agreements have been reached. In a large multi-plant company there may, however, be some similar problems of allowing for different circumstances and practice between different establishments of the company. British Leyland has negotiated a framework agreement which provides an example of how change may be accommodated in a multi-plant organisation. The section of the agreement headed 'The management of change' specifies a number of clauses which should be included in negotiating plant agreements and which by no means outline a tightly-defined formulation of either side's right to effect change. The agreement goes a step beyond many others in that it proposes local codification of current custom and practice and there is a *status quo* clause which includes reference to established custom and practice. An agreement between one engineering company and the AUEW, signed in January 1972, includes the following *status quo* clause:

> 'Where the management takes a decision which is within the framework of an existing agreement or an established practice there shall be no obligation upon the management to postpone the implementation of that decision until agreement has been reached or the procedure has been exhausted. This gives management the right to maintain the *status quo*.

> 'On the other hand, where the management wishes to implement a decision which would mean departing from an existing agreement or an established practice, and the worker concerned objects to that decision, the management shall be obliged to reach agreement or exhaust the procedure before implementing the decision. This gives the workers the right to maintain the *status quo*'.

This is close to the wording of the EEF's proposal in 1970 with the addition of the final sentence of each paragraph.

223 Formulations of this sort are dependent upon a common interpretation of what constitutes an agreement and more particularly an established practice. Scheduling or codification of current custom and practice as proposed in the British Leyland agreement can be a useful measure of clarification but only if there is a good mutual understanding about the purpose to be achieved. Otherwise unnecessary argument might develop – unnecessary because either no occasion for change arises or if it does arise it will be necessary at that time to reach an understanding about the conditions which will allow the change to be carried through effectively. An understanding may in fact prove easier to reach in relation to specific proposals than in relation to hypothetical future contingencies.

224 Higher management may not always be aware of practice at shop floor level. Where the work group is strong, informal understandings and practices between workers and lower management often operate independently of any written or unwritten procedure in which higher management and shop stewards play a positive role. Understandings may evolve between the workgroup and lower management about the conduct of certain day-to-day affairs. A deficiency in control systems which leads higher management to act in good faith in accordance with a *status quo* formulation but in ignorance of and contrary to understandings developed between the workforce and lower management at shop floor level may lead to difficulties both with the workforce and between senior and junior management.

225 *Status quo* clauses seek to establish that change will not be made before agreement is reached or procedure exhausted. Retrospection clauses guarantee the operation of agreed terms from the time when the change is made. The exhaustion of procedure without agreement marks the moment under both types of clause when the parties have to consider whether to take independent action. A *status quo* clause should by its nature defer the occasion for strike action but is sometimes traded for a separate clause prohibiting strike action whilst any issue is 'in procedure'. A retrospection clause commonly includes a no-strike provision as an integral part of the clause. An example from a recently negotiated procedure agreement in an engineering company states:

> 'The trade unions and an employee or employees involved in a dispute will undertake that there will be no stoppage of work or departure from normal working practice in return for assurance of retrospection of an agreement under the terms of "the procedure".'

Another engineering company sought to combine the idea of discussion before action with a safeguard against long delay by adding to its *status quo* proposals a provision which stated:

> 'If the circumstances demand that action be taken before formal agreement is reached or the procedure exhausted, but after due discussions, the decision shall be implemented without prejudice to either side pending the outcome of the procedural discussions'.

The unions would not agree to this.

226 The term *status quo* and the intensity of the discussions to which it has given rise are particularly associated with the engineering industry but the underlying issues concerning management functions and the ways in which their exercise may be modified as a consequence of jointly agreed procedures are found in all industries and services. Clauses explicitly dealing with the subject are however found only in a minority of agreements (see para 212). The existence or absence of such clauses is no guide to actual practice.

227 An industry-wide agreement in the textile industry includes a specific *status quo* clause:

> 'Where an issue arises upon a proposed change in agreed wage levels
> or working conditions no change should be made until the issue
> has been dealt with in accordance with the procedure laid down in the
> Agreement'.

The employers' association reported that it could not recall an instance when this clause had been invoked and one of the district associations confirmed that this was the case so far in its constituency. The employers meet no hostility when introducing new machinery and any points of detail the unions wish to raise are discussed at a later stage.

228 In many industries, of which printing and docks are good examples, prior discussion with unions before management action is taken is not attributable to explicit *status quo* clauses but to a high degree of union organisation and to the consequent development of the practice of negotiation and joint agreement as the effective prerequisite of management action over a wide range of issues. In the London Enclosed Docks, for example, holidays, sick pay, amenities, safety and training are all subject to negotiation and although manning is formally specifically retained in the written agreement within the prerogative of management, in practice it is subject to negotiation.

229 One of the objectives of a *status quo* clause is to prevent a *fait accompli* before discussions can take place. This is also an objective of consultation agreements. The *status quo* implications are clearly apparent in an agreement between the British Federation of Master Printers and the National Graphical Association, signed in 1972. Under 'New processes and changes in methods of production' it is stated that:

> 'The parties to this agreement agree that there should be early
> consultation and full co-operation between employees and all unions
> concerned in the adoption and development of new processes and
> new types of machine'.

Where management is committed to consult with unions, as in the agreement just quoted, and the unions are powerful it is evident that there is only a difference in degree between consultation and negotiation. Discussion about the introduction of new machinery will inevitably develop into negotiation and action will depend on the outcome.

230 In nationalisation statutes it is standard practice to place an obligation on the management to seek to establish with appropriate unions machinery for consultation and negotiation. Such machinery has been established in all the nationalised industries. Consultation and negotiation are usually kept separate in form but in practice the distinction is often blurred.

231 Local factors including management and union policy, historical tradition, technology and size of establishment all affect attitudes and practice in evolving working understandings about the use of procedures. In some industries, there are special arrangements to provide for interim management decisions to avoid interruption of production. One example is found in the shop stewards demarcation disputes procedure of May 1969 in shipbuilding. This allows management to make temporary decisions to ensure completion of work on time, but invokes the procedure subsequently to sort out any continuing conflict. The importance of avoiding interruptions to production is particularly evident in continuous process industries and production requirements for large-scale change in the capital equipment used put a premium on the avoidance of delay. In the steel industry the practice of 'working under protest' has been commonly used to allow work to proceed while discussions were taking place.

232 In small establishments where communications can be quick and easy and the controlling management is well placed to know actual practice at the workplace there need be few arguments about the use of procedure. Procedural norms are often built up by custom and practice over a long period. The management and unions in a commercial printing firm employing 240 workers both claimed to have a harmonious common understanding of how their procedures should and did operate though little was laid down in writing. Similar views were expressed elsewhere, often in the local establishments of large concerns where there was freedom for the parties to establish their operating relationship, sometimes within the framework of guidelines set out in a company or industry-wide agreement.

233 The questions outlined in the opening paragraph of this chapter appear to call for answers by way of definition. Yet where agreed definition has been attempted it has often either not been possible to reach agreement or the formally agreed provisions have been at variance with actual practice. Partly this is due to the constant change which makes definition except in the broadest terms out-of-date almost as soon as it is made : the matters subject to joint discussion and the readiness of the parties to use the method of joint discussion constantly evolve out of the experience and practice of joint discussion. Partly it is due to trying to find national formulae to fit a wide variety of local practice. Partly it is due to seeking to subject to general rule decisions which will depend on the policy and power of individuals and organisations in particular circumstances. The answers have to be sought within individual companies and establishments. The commitment of the parties to the use of procedure reflects their convictions, their policies, their strength and the pressures they are subject to.

8 The contribution of procedures

234 The Donovan Commission saw the main requirement for remedying 'the central defect in British industrial relations' as the development of company and factory-wide agreements establishing procedures for the conduct of collective bargaining, for dealing with grievances, disciplinary matters and redundancy, for regulating the position of shop stewards and for promoting joint discussion on safety measures. These objectives were to guide the policies of companies, of trade unions and employers' associations, of the State and of the new agency, the Commission on Industrial Relations, which was to be created to promote them. Would experience since 1968 modify that vision?

235 Perhaps the emphasis on procedural reform in the Donovan report fostered misconceptions about what could be attained by this means. Good procedures cannot ensure that all disputed issues and in particular major pay issues will be settled peacefully. Some of the most spectacular disputes follow meticulous observance of preliminary procedures. Decisions on substantive issues like pay levels are matters of policy and procedures do not determine policy decisions. They are the means through which they are carried out.

236 Does this suggest that better procedures have a very minor role to play in the improvement of industrial relations? Certainly improved procedures will not solve the major economic, political and social problems giving rise to industrial conflict in an inflationary era. If the state of industrial relations is assessed in terms of those conflicts which provide the major news coverage of industrial relations, then the contribution to be made by improved procedures may well appear to be a fringe benefit. But most people's own experience of industrial relations is very different from what they read on that subject in their newspapers or hear from the news bulletins. And even those who do become involved in major conflict spend most of their working life with other preoccupations. It would be unfortunate if the very real contribution which good procedures can make to the improvement of day to day industrial relations at the workplace were to be discounted because improved procedures will not eliminate major conflicts of interest or determine which interest shall prevail.

237 Procedures for dealing with matters affecting the interests of employees exist in all places where people are employed. They are a necessary part of the operating arrangements. Where there is no negotiation with

representatives of employees they are a sole management responsibility even though not always explicitly recognised or very successfully discharged. The procedure may need to be deduced from discovering what is the customary practice with little in the way of formal arrangements to point to. Not that the effectiveness of procedures, whether determined solely by the management or established by joint agreement, can be assessed from the formal arrangements. It depends much more on the general quality of industrial relations in the establishment.

238 The Industrial Relations Act 1971 contained provisions for the introduction of enforceable procedures at the instance of one of the parties, subject to a prescribed process of official investigation and judicial pronouncement. The provisions were never operated. The idea that the procedural cart could pull the horse of good industrial relations did not appeal either to employers or to unions. Yet the same belief that behaviour can be made to conform to prescribed rules, just because there are prescribed rules, often underlies charges of breaches of negotiated procedures. Industry-wide negotiated procedures may prescribe the steps to be followed when an 'issue' arises in a member firm. What in fact happens in any particular firm may be influenced by a nationally negotiated procedure but will depend essentially on the state of domestic industrial relations as reflected in the domestic procedures which take the impact of local issues. This does not mean that industry-wide procedures are bound to be ineffective. They can give guidelines to local negotiations, establish principles to which both sides can appeal and provide outside assistance when local negotiations fail to resolve an issue. Nor does it mean that domestic procedures can be relied on to be effective. They can only be effective if they reflect a generally sound state of industrial relations and a determination by both sides to use agreed procedures.

239 Commitment to enter into and make the fullest use of jointly agreed procedures poses different but related problems and opportunities to managements and unions. For management there is a loss of sole discretion and authority in some aspects of running the business. This is a renunciation which is made, and can only be made, where there is effective organisation of employees asserting a right to a say in how matters affecting their interests are run. There can be a return in goodwill and more effective operation. For unions jointly agreed procedures establish in the interests of their members constraints on managerial authority. They also imply for the unions a renunciation of complete freedom and discretion to use their strength as they think best in order to press a case. For this reason a powerful union may, as we saw in examining redundancy procedures, decline to enter into a procedural commitment but prefer to reserve its position; it may, where it effectively controls some aspect of running the business, such as recruitment or work organisation, decline to bring the subject within the ambit of jointly-agreed arrangements. For both management and unions jointly agreed procedures betoken a renunciation of unilateral authority.

240 Renunciation of unilateral authority in favour of jointly agreed arrangements follows a successful challenge by adequate strength. It may be assisted by a conviction that the new regime will in practice be more effective but such a conviction can only be held when both parties have the strength to make a contribution to the authority which is to be exercised. Jointly agreed procedures are bargains in the sense that they represent a deal. Whether they are bargains in the sense that they represent good value depends on the parties.

241 Agreements may represent the terms subscribed to from necessity and without enthusiasm by mutually suspicious enemies or they may represent the foundation for a genuinely desired and expected co-operation. Jointly-agreed procedures need mutual trust and goodwill for their successful operation. Where they have been conceded reluctantly by a management unreconciled to the union's role, or accepted as providing useful tactical dispositions by employee representatives ideologically opposed to the concept of co-operation, jointly agreed procedures can provide frequent occasions for disputes over interpretation and accusations of breaches of agreed arrangements. The wording and the formal requirements of procedures rarely give a closely accurate indication of actual behaviour. This is so both in places where disregard of procedure is seen as evidence of the poor state of industrial relations and in places where flexibility in the interpretation and operation of procedures is seen as evidence of good industrial relations.

242 Can it be inferred then that the actual structure and terms of procedures are unimportant and that all that matters is that there should be mutual goodwill? Mutual goodwill is certainly an indispensable ingredient but it is not a whole recipe. If the goodwill is to be effectively expressed and sustained in difficult times the procedures need to be well designed. An omnibus grievance procedure requires that every 'issue' should follow its prescribed route halting at the appropriate stages. This may not go to the right places or travel at the right speed for some types of issue which require specialised consideration and speedy resolution. One way of dealing with such a problem is to by-pass the procedure by *ad hoc* action. A better way is to design a procedure to suit the circumstances.

243 A jointly-agreed procedure is the agreed method of dealing with a problem in which both the management and the employees have an interest. It may be a method for seeking to reconcile differing interests, for example over a pay question, or of dealing with business in a way which avoids occasions for conflict, for example by establishing the rules for selection for training, promotion, the performance of rostered duties or temporary transfer to an outstation. Joint discussions should aim to identify the kind of problems which occur in the course of work and how they can best be brought under consideration and disposed of. The study of model procedures and of the experience of other organisations can be very helpful but procedures need to be tailor-made to fit the circumstances in which they are to operate. Often a specialised procedure has its origins through being separated from a more general procedure which experience showed to be not well adapted to handling that particular problem efficiently.

244   If the conclusion is that procedures need to be well-planned, well-designed, well understood and generally adhered to does it follow that they should be worked out in detail and committed to writing? Written procedures have the advantage that the process of drawing them up promotes discussion of the points likely to arise and an agreed text reduces the possibilities of later misunderstanding. This can be of particular importance following changes in personnel amongst those responsible for operating the procedures. A written text is also useful for disseminating knowledge of the procedure among all those who may be affected by its operation or required to abide by its provisions. It provides a common basis and reference point for consideration of change and amendment. These are solid advantages which in general it is desirable to secure. But there are some qualifications. A written text expresses the formal position which can be changed by a formal amendment. But the process of change is gradual and often develops through custom and practice long before it is acknowledged through formal agreement. Custom and practice before it becomes consolidated often provides an experimental area for trying out developments without commitment; it can be a supplementary agency for dealing with special cases; it can cope with a mass of detail unsuitable for registering in an agreement of wide general application.

245   Formal and informal procedures are not alternative and mutually exclusive arrangements. They exist side by side and can usefully complement each other if there is a good mutual understanding between the parties about the operation of the system. Formal written procedures should have all the authority of mutual agreements which both parties are committed to uphold. Against that background it is always open to parties to operate procedures flexibly, to depart on occasion from the strict letter of procedural requirements, if that suits convenience and commonsense, provided always that modifications to secure the most practical day to day operation are as much the subject of informal joint agreement as the written terms are the subject of formal agreement.

246 Many managers and union officials extol the virtues of informality and shy away from written commitments. They express a genuine conviction that formal agreements are restrictive and could prejudice a relationship which is based on mutual trust. One of the most impressive of smoothly operating procedures observed during the inquiries was in a medium sized establishment where little was available by way of written procedures but managers, shop stewards and workpeople all had a clear understanding and acceptance of exactly what to do or to expect in the handling of problems arising at work. In many cases, however, a preference for informality stems from a reluctance to accept commitments, and from a belief that what has become firmly established informally is somehow capable of being readily changed.

247 The idea that informality preserves a freedom of action which is lost if procedures are committed to writing ignores the fact that the effective constraint on freedom of action arises from the strength of the parties. It is perfectly true that a strong party may make concessions on a discretionary basis and without commitment. It is however equally true that a weak party finds informality and *ad hoc* action an excuse for yielding readily to pressure while safeguarding appearances. It is precisely where there is no established mode of doing business that the opportunities for exploiting weakness by constant pressure are greatest. Written procedures limit the area of uncertainty. They strengthen the defences of management, unions and employees against arbitrary and unpredictable action.

248 Despite the qualifications and the exceptional cases, the balance of advantage appeared to be clearly in favour of formal written procedures. This is not to suggest that it would be wise to try to constitutionalise everything. The tendency is for formal procedures to be extended but the process should be one which from time to time registers clearly established change rather than one which seeks to achieve a comprehensive and essentially static definition in an evolving situation.

249 Well established procedures operating to good effect are found where both parties are strong and recognise their respective roles in pursuing the particular interests they represent within the context of the common interests they share. Established procedures are the practical expression and tangible evidence of the parties' understanding of their mutual relationship. Both sides are concerned to uphold the procedures which embody the positions they have achieved in settling how they will conduct business. It is a concern which transcends their interest in a transient case.

250 Whether procedures are in fact successful in containing business as intended depends on whether they were well designed in the first place and whether they have been adapted to meet changing needs. A commitment by both sides to abide by and uphold a procedure is a condition for its success but defence of the procedure needs to be matched by a readiness to change it if necessary. The commitment is to the procedural method and principle rather than to maintaining a particular system against all change. A procedure is only useful if it corresponds to reality and fulfils its purpose. Breaches of procedure are a signal to both parties to examine whether the procedure is adequate to its task.

251 Procedural malfunction may be due not to defects in the procedure itself but to faults in the situation with which it has to cope. A number of cases were observed where the payments system gave rise to so many anomalies and problems that a conventional grievance procedure was overwhelmed by the burden of complaints. In such cases the procedural arrangements might be improved, for example by setting up a specialised procedure for dealing promptly with pay issues, but before that course is adopted it needs to be considered whether it would not merely be alleviating symptoms rather than treating causes. One of the useful functions of a grievance procedure is to indicate where troubles giving rise to industrial relations problems need to be tackled. It may not just be the fuse or the safety valve that needs attention.

252 Another indication that something more fundamental than procedural matters needs to be reviewed is provided by the controversy over *status quo*. A firm commitment to the use of agreed procedures is central to the maintenance of good industrial relations. But wrangles about whether or not procedures are applicable betoken a state of affairs where procedures, instead of following and embodying the achievement of a good understanding on mutual relationships, are being used to pursue an unresolved conflict about what those relationships should be. That is an antecedent issue which needs to be resolved by other means. It is resolved primarily by the strength of the parties and by the policies they pursue in adjusting to their situation. In establishments where unions are strongly organised and the parties have evolved a close working relationship *status quo* often goes unmentioned in formal agreements. Unions see no need to make formal provision for joint discussion before action is taken in places where they are confident that the management would think it right, or at any rate prudent, to clear their lines with the unions before embarking on action which could give rise to a dispute. In establishments where employee organisation is weak the existence of a *status quo* clause in a national agreement is unlikely to make much difference to the way in which affairs are conducted. In so far as the *status quo* principle is intended to reinforce the doctrine that procedures should be observed it meets with general approval; in so far as it is advocated in the belief that it will extend union power or resisted in the belief that it will undermine managerial authority it is something of a symbolic controversy reflecting hopes and fears which are in fact realised or dispelled by the power realities of the local situation.

253 In their booklet on disputes procedures the CBI observe that the *status quo* issue tends to disappear when joint consultation is 'practised with goodwill' and also note the tendency of consultations 'of a purely advisory character' to merge into negotiations (see above – para 205). The formal distinction between consultation and negotiation is that consultation involves an exchange of information and views before action is taken by management whereas negotiation normally requires either joint agreement or exhaustion of procedure before action is taken. Management action following exhaustion of procedure may not of course give rise to counter action; on the other hand there is no guarantee that management action following consultation may not be met by counter action if it is considered that insufficient account has been taken of the views expressed. In both processes discussion precedes action. What follows thereafter is more likely to be determined by the strength of the parties, the state of their relations with each other and their appraisal of the situation than by a nice distinction between consultation and negotiation. Joint consultation and negotiation are of course themselves carried out through procedures and where they are well established as the accepted way of conducting business they provide a more comprehensive, sensitive and adaptable safeguard against unwarranted arbitrary action than can be achieved through specific *status quo* clauses.

254 Where parties accept the principle of joint regulation of matters of joint concern procedures provide the machinery to carry through the policies informed by that principle. They are an expression of such policies but they do not create them. They determine how things shall be done but not what shall be done. Yet how things are done is of such importance in industrial relations that the achievement of satisfactory working procedures becomes a major policy end in itself. What are the conditions of success?

255 Clearly a desire to establish jointly agreed procedures is a prime condition. But such a policy aim can only be pursued where employees have the organised strength to make an accommodation desirable. It is the potential for conflict which generates the need for agreement. It is the organisation of employees which makes it possible. Agreement requires at least two parties and agreements with a body of employees need a representative organisation which can speak on their behalf and which has the strength both to advance their views to some effect and to see that agreements entered into are observed. Acceptance of the trade union role is the foundation on which jointly agreed procedures are built. Whether or not much is achieved will depend not only on having parties with power to make effective agreements but also on the quality of the representatives of both sides and of the relationship they establish.

256 The scope of procedures is as wide as the scope of joint discussion and agreement. Procedures are the follow-through of joint agreement. If employee representatives raise a question about how some particular bit of business is handled and agreement is reached on how it will be handled in future then an agreed procedure is born. If management wish to carry through a change in a method of operation and agreement is reached on how it will be done the result is an agreed procedure either short-term or with continuing effect.

257 It was partly because of the wide ramifications of procedures that the voluntary notification of procedural agreements to the Department of Employment, which was introduced following a recommendation of the Donovan Commission, proved to be of limited value. It was the immense scope of the subject which prompted the remark by an industrialist, already quoted, to the effect that notification of the jointly-agreed procedures in his company would require the submission of loads of minutes of joint meetings extending over decades. Added to the network of procedures developed over long periods of joint discussion is the constant procedural adaptation arising from changes in custom and practice. The proliferation of procedures might appear to lead to confusion rather than to the clarity and certainty which agreed procedures aim to achieve.

258 There are several reasons why procedural complexity need not be perplexing to those involved. One fundamental reason is that procedures in the sense of rules governing behaviour are often not experienced as procedures but simply accepted as the way things are done. They are learned and practised as an integral part of the job and the environment. Much more noticeable than what exists is any change in the established way of doing things. Even so, changes are often made without any great consciousness of procedural revision but simply as agreed or tolerated adaptations to circumstances, the development of a new custom and practice. Where, however, existing practice, and more emphatically, proposed changes, do give rise to problems a unifying, simplifying, overriding procedure for handling all forms of procedural change is provided by the central negotiating machinery. Much of the procedural output of those decades of minutes of joint meetings is not so much the construction of imposing new edifices as works of adaptation, extension, demolition, repair and maintenance to the existing buildings.

259 Because the maintenance and development of procedures is a continuing process that does not mean that it must also be one of living from hand to mouth and being pushed along by events. Procedures should be planned to deal with known problems. They should cover the familiar contingencies of grievances, disputes and discipline but they should also be designed to deal with particular aspects of running the business which are known to give rise to industrial relations problems. Comprehensive procedures require in the first place a comprehensive review of industrial relations problems. The best outcome of such a review is the elimination of the cause of the problem but where that is not possible it needs to be considered whether an agreed procedure can be devised which will contain the problem and ease its handling. During the inquiries there were discussions with two firms which had in recent years carried out major reviews of this sort followed by major procedural reforms. In both cases the management and unions were highly satisfied with the results.

260 Major procedural changes in industrial relations are often brought about by pressures arising from other developments. Technical innovation, expansion or decline, mergers, changes in organisation, in products, in production methods, in pay systems may lead to a general review of the industrial relations system. They will in any event have industrial relations aspects which will need to be taken into account as an integral part of the planning of the proposed changes and which may well require modification of existing procedures.

261 A planned control of procedures should not however be confined to the relatively infrequent occasions when a complete restructuring is to be carried out. The way in which existing procedures are operating needs to be kept under joint review. In the course of use changes in the operation of procedures are often made for reasons of practical convenience, often as adaptations to other changes in the organisation. When over a period the cumulative effect of such changes has resulted in an actual practice markedly different from the formally agreed provisions it should be considered whether the agreement should not be brought up to date to take account of the changes which have occurred. Nobody would want to be constantly revising procedures which should represent an element of stability in the conduct of affairs. But a periodic stocktaking to make sure that procedures are fulfilling their purpose satisfactorily is more likely to maintain their effectiveness than is a reluctance to acknowledge signs of obsolescence.

262 The negotiating machinery provides an accepted means for dealing with problems which call for immediate attention. It needs a conscious policy drive to see that solutions to immediate problems are followed by a review of the situation which gave rise to the problem and the institution of any procedural measures which might be indicated. It needs an even stronger initiative in the absence of any direct prompting from immediate problems nevertheless to keep the adequacy of procedural arrangements under review. Procedures are not a substitute for policy but a close scrutiny of procedures has a double advantage. First, an examination of how things are done can be a good starting point for considering why they are so done and whether they should continue to be so done. Secondly, it can show whether what are believed to be existing policies are in fact carried through into actual practice.

263 An oversight of the operation of procedures requires the maintenance of reasonable records and statistics to show the incidence and character of the business transacted and the results. The need for adequate documentation for dealing with appeals has already been noted. The operation of procedures is an important aspect of running a business and needs the same attention to business efficiency as the conduct of other operations. The scope for such attention was shown when the law on unfair dismissals caused a general review and reform of dismissal procedures. Procedures are concerned with how things are done and are primarily concerned that they should be done wisely, humanely, acceptably but these primary aims are assisted if the procedures are operated efficiently with proper records and servicing. It is important that they should be well known and understood. Both parties have a responsibility for publicising agreed procedures. Induction training courses should outline the procedures in operation and industrial relations training courses should include both instruction in the proper operation of procedures and critical discussion of their purpose and effectiveness.

264 It may be observed that practically every general statement made about procedures can be matched by a statement of a different and often quite opposite character. On the one hand procedures embody the agreed rules which both parties should uphold and require to be observed both in encounters with each other and with their own members and masters; on the other they are essentially an instrument to serve the interests of the parties and need to be operated flexibly and with commonsense. On the one hand their success depends on goodwill and mutual trust between the parties; on the other they will only be successful if each side clearly understands and vigorously prosecutes the interests which it represents. The parties are at once both collaborators and opponents. Again, procedures need to be clearly thought out, authoritatively expressed and generally understood and these aims are best served if procedures are treated with an appropriate formality and expressed in writing; but informal action outside the constraints of formal agreements is commonly felt to be a necessary lubricant for the smooth operation of the established machinery and is often the precursor of change and reform. Procedures should be comprehensive; but they may need to be specialised. They are of the first importance; but they are merely the subordinate agents of policy. They must express current practice; but they rarely do so completely. They must endure; but they must be changed. They must be humane; they must be efficient.

265 Such many-sided characteristics are not surprising in arrangements designed to contain and regulate the flow of changing and enduring, of shared and differing interests in a working community. The procedural patterns reflect the distinctive roles and responsibilities of employers and their employees in matters of common interest and the central negotiating machinery provides the focal point for creating, sustaining, co-ordinating and modifying procedures. Where there is a firm commitment to the principles and practice of joint working by both sides the practical measures to give effect to jointly agreed solutions of problems are consequential.

266 Was the Donovan Commission right in emphasising the importance of domestic procedural agreements? The limitations of what can be expected from jointly agreed procedures must be recognised. They will not solve economic conflicts of interest though they can help to reduce the risk of damaging misunderstandings and to ensure that all possibilities of reaching agreement are fully explored and reasonably considered. They will only work if both parties genuinely wish to conduct their affairs by joint agreement and are willing to limit their powers to take unilateral action. They cannot be imposed on unwilling parties though third parties can give valuable advice and assistance both in the creation of suitable procedures and in the resolution of particular problems. Procedures will only be as effective as the strength and competence of the parties permits. They will only be as good as the policies they express.

267 Within these limitations jointly-agreed procedures can establish accepted standards of conduct and influence behaviour. They can give early warning of developing problems and provide experience in devising methods of dealing with them. They put a premium on rationality and fairness and a discount on arbitrary action. They can affect the whole style and tone and morale of an enterprise. These are important benefits. Good procedures are not the answer to all industrial relations problems but an essential instrument for carrying into effect a sound industrial relations policy.